Mo

Dwarf
Rabbits

How to Take Care of Them and Understand Them

With color photos by Monika Wegler
and drawings by György Jankovics

Consulting Editor:
Lucia Vriends-Parent

BARRON'S

Contents

Rabbits enjoy eating vegetables, fruits, and herbs every day. Greens, however, should be offered fresh and only in small quantities.

Preface

Dwarf rabbits are small and cuddly. With their round heads, large bright eyes, and cute little ears, they touch a great many hearts, inevitably rousing there a desire to own and look after one of these stuffed toys come to life. If this love story turns out badly, the disappointment is enormous. This new Pet Owner's Manual will help you prevent an unhappy outcome. Monika Wegler, an expert on rabbits, explains here what kind of care and treatment a dwarf rabbit must have in order to develop properly. This involves more than just providing the proper food and observing the rules of basic health care. Only by becoming thoroughly familiar with your pet's body language and the sounds it uses to communicate can you avoid mistakes in dealing with it.

On the How To pages, instructions and drawings describe what you need to keep in mind when buying a cage and accessories, looking after your pet, or raising young dwarf rabbits. Because all the directions are easy to follow, children also will learn quickly to understand their dwarf rabbit's needs and to take care of it on their own. Expert advice, informative drawings, and high-quality color photos taken by the author herself make this book an indispensable companion for everyone who owns a dwarf rabbit.

The author and the editors of Barron's Pet Owner's Manuals wish you a great deal of pleasure with your dwarf rabbit.

*D*warf rabbits are soft, cute, and downright huggable. No wonder children, in particular, are crazy about them. However, you need to know as much as possible about these animals' care and behavior if you want your pets to stay healthy and bring you pleasure for many years to come.

Please read the "Important Information" on page 63.

Before Buying a Dwarf Rabbit

With its round button eyes, chubby cheeks, and soft fur, a dwarf rabbit looks so sweet and appealing that you want to keep picking it up and petting it. Cuddling alone is not enough, however. If you want to enjoy owning a healthy rabbit for many years to come, you need to know something about its behavior and basic living requirements. First, make sure that a dwarf rabbit is really the right pet for you.

Ten Points to Help You Decide

1. Given the proper care, a dwarf rabbit can live to be 10 years old. You will have to look after the animal throughout its entire life.

2. Feeding and taking care of the dwarf rabbit require at least one hour a day.

3. An open enclosure in the yard or on the terrace is best for the animal's health during the warm months.

4. To keep a dwarf rabbit indoors, you need a room that is not furnished with a hard-to-clean wall-to-wall carpet and expensive pieces of furniture (see page 17).

5. A dwarf rabbit needs plenty of space in which to run about, but attempts at housebreaking are not always successful (see page 16). Will this offend your sense of tidiness?

6. If you cannot take your rabbit along on vacation, you will have to make provisions for its care ahead of time.

7. Dwarf rabbits can get sick, too. You will have to devote time to its care and pay the veterinarian's bills.

8. If you already have a pet, it should be able to get along with the dwarf rabbit; otherwise, you will have to take the time to help the animals adjust to each other (see pages 24 and 25).

9. Have you checked with your family to see whether everyone shares your desire to get a dwarf rabbit?

10. Find out ahead of time whether any member of your family has an allergic reaction to rabbit fur. If there is any doubt, ask your doctor before proceeding with your plans.

Happier Alone or Together?

You can keep a single dwarf rabbit if you are able to find a little time to spend with your pet several times a day. This means not only feeding it and seeing to its basic needs, but also petting the animal. In addition, if its spirits are to remain high, it needs sufficient diversion and exercise. If you want to do your dwarf rabbit a favor, try keeping two of them. Rabbits enjoy being with other members of their species, because it is their nature to live in large groups, or colonies.

Two does (females) will get along especially well if they grow up together from the outset. Females from the same litter will get along best.

A Jamora harlequin, five weeks old. These dwarf Angoras are an attractive new breed that is still a rarity.

A giant rabbit and a Siamese dwarf rabbit.
These rabbits are six weeks old. Only the difference in ear length is an indicator that someday they will be different in size.

Female.

Male.

In the male, the sexual orifice, with the testicles located to its right and left, is round in shape; in the female it is an elongated oval.

Two bucks (males) will get along together only for the first few months. With the onset of sexual maturity (at the age of about four months), contests over rank will begin, and the animals can cause serious injuries to one another.

A pair will produce young continually, and you will have to find a place to house the offspring. You can avoid this problem by having the buck neutered by your veterinarian.

Male or Female?

If you intend to keep your pet indoors, a doe is a better choice. A male would have to be neutered (at approximately four months of age) because it usually is too fidgety. Moreover, males will spray urine (to mark their territory and their mate), which has a pervasive sweetish odor and is difficult to remove.

Sexing a rabbit: Determining the sex of a young rabbit is not a simple matter; it is best left to the breeder or pet store owner, who will have ex-

To determine the sex of your rabbit, hold the animal on your lap in this position.

perience in this area. In an adult male animal, the testicles, which lie left and right of the round sexual orifice, are an infallible indicator. The penis will be exposed if you carefully pull the sexual orifice open by pressing down gently, toward the abdomen, with two fingers (see drawing, left).

Females have a narrow, almost slit-like orifice that looks like a thin line running toward the anus. The distance between the sexual orifice and the anus is markedly shorter in the female than in the male.

Purebred Dwarf or Crossbred?

Young rabbits are small and cute. Only the purchaser of a purebred, or pedigreed, dwarf can be certain that the animal will still be small when it is full-grown. The most reliable indicators of the dwarf rabbit's adult size are the ears; the longer they are, the larger the animal will grow. An eight-week-old rabbit with ears 2¾ to 3 inches (7–8 cm) long will certainly weigh between 5 pounds 8 ounces and 8 pounds 13 ounces (2.5–4 kg) when fully grown. With ears 4 inches (10 cm) long, the animal later will be a giant rabbit, no longer able to fit in an indoor cage. Other reliable distinguishing marks are listed in the table on page 7.

A note about crossbreds, or mongrels: They are available in all shades and in extremely attractive colors, and if you are not interested in breeding, a crossbred can give you just as much pleasure as a purebred dwarf rabbit.

Dwarf Rabbits as Presents for Children

These appealing little rabbits frequently are purchased for children. Often, however, the buyer fails to take into account how quickly children's lives and interests change. After some length of time, the animal is often neglected and left to endure a sad exis-

How to Recognize a Purebred Dwarf Rabbit

	Purebred Dwarf Rabbit	Dwarf Crossbred, Other Rabbits
Ears:	Small, close-set ears, rounded at the tips. Ideal length in a full-grown dwarf: 1¾–2¼ in (4.5–5.5 cm).	Longer, set farther apart, more pointed at the tips. Length, depending on size, 2¾–4 in (7–10 cm) and more.
Build:	Cobby, cylindrical body; short back line and legs.	Body more slender and elongated; legs longer.
Head:	Seems overly large and hefty in relation to body; broad skull, with roof of the skull strongly arched.	Of normal size in relation to body; in general, more elongated and narrower.
Neck:	Narrowing at neck scarcely visible; the head seems to sit right on the body.	Narrowing at neck plainly visible.
Eyes:	Large, slightly protruding; bones clearly curved.	In keeping with body size, less prominent; bones only slightly curved.
Fur color:	Only the standard colors and markings (see pages 46 and 47).	All fur colors and markings are possible.
Weight:	In a full-grown dwarf: 1½–3⅓ lbs (0.7–1.5 kg).	Depending on genes, up to 11 lbs (5 kg) and more.

tence in its cage, assuming it is not dropped off at an animal shelter. Some pet rabbits are even placed outdoors and abandoned. It is up to parents to educate and guide their children so that such an outcome can be prevented.
• Never give a dwarf rabbit to children of preschool age.
• Never assume that your child can take sole responsibility for the animal. If that is what you intend, it is better not to get the pet.
• If your child's sudden wish for a pet takes you by surprise, the desire may be motivated by something other than genuine love of animals. A child who feels lonely may long for some object to cuddle, but an animal should not be made to suffer in this role.

Note: Before considering the purchase of rabbits, check with local authorities. Ordinances in certain areas restrict or even prohibit the keeping of rabbits.

Where to Get a Dwarf Rabbit

Ask a pet store owner whether he or she can obtain a purebred dwarf rabbit for you. Pet stores and the pet sections of large department stores usually sell dwarf crossbreds (see page 6).

Rabbit breeders' clubs (addresses of these organizations can usually be found in the telephone book) occasionally have purebred animals for sale.

What to Look for When Buying a Rabbit

Age when purchased: A dwarf rabbit can be sold when it is eight weeks old. It switches completely to solid food before this time, at six weeks of age, but during this often critical period it should be left with its mother. Do not buy an animal less than eight weeks old! The risk that a tiny four- or five-week-old baby rabbit will become ill is quite high.

It should be healthy: A healthy rabbit always has smooth, shiny fur. It is frisky and lively, unless it happens to be resting. Depending on its temperament, it will jump timidly into a corner or hop up curiously to sniff at your hand. In any event, it will move its ears back and forth and show interest in whatever is going on around it.

A properly equipped indoor cage, large enough to accommodate two dwarf rabbits.

What to watch out for: A sick animal usually sits listlessly in a corner, does not react to noises, and stares straight ahead with dull eyes. Other signs of illness are the following:
- Inflamed and watery eyes.
- Frequent sneezing or coughing.
- Nasal discharge.
- A hard, taut abdomen.
- Shaggy, dull fur, possibly even with bare patches and with feces smeared on the abdomen and around the anus.

Location of the Cage
A cage that provides sufficient room for the rabbit and the equipment it needs is not exactly small (see "How To: Setting up the Cage," page 10). Nevertheless, it cannot simply be placed wherever it will be least in the way. Rather it should be in a spot where your pet will feel comfortable and will not become ill. The cage is properly placed if it is:
- In a quiet room—rabbits have a keen sense of hearing, and noise from a loud radio, shouting children, and constant running back and forth past the cage are stressful for your pet. A television set in the same room also will bother the rabbit, which hears frequencies in the supersonic range and finds them painful.
- Away from drafty air—do not set the cage on the floor; instead, place it on a sturdy stand or a table where no one can knock it off. Always close the cage securely. When airing the cage, make sure that it does not stand in a draft (cover it if need be). Drafts are harmful to rabbits; they often cause colds and other related illnesses.
- In a room with moderate temperature—keep the cage far away from radiators and stoves. In summer, make sure the sun does not shine directly on the cage. Rabbits are not comfortable in high heat and overheated, dry rooms.

Only two weeks old and already so inquisitive.

- In a bright spot, but not in the sun—in dark rooms or in winter, turn on a light during the daytime if necessary. Rabbits' vital rhythms are influenced by light, and overly long periods of darkness will make your pet lethargic.

In the photo:
The little nest box provides safety and security to this two-week-old dwarf rabbit. It rarely leaves its nest at this stage, but in the third week it will venture out more often.

HOW–TO
Setting Up the Cage

An indoor rabbit spends a great deal of time in its cage. Consequently, the rabbit's quarters have to be both sufficiently large and properly equipped. These How To pages will explain what is essential for your pet's comfort when it is confined. If you have a yard, you can also build an outdoor pen for your rabbit; this section will show you how.

The Right Cage
You can purchase your rabbit's cage in a pet store or in the pet section of a large department store. Cages come in various sizes and styles—an example is shown in the photo on page 8. When buying a rabbit cage, keep the following in mind:

Plastic tray on the bottom: The tray should be at least 28 inches (70 cm) long, 18 inches (45 cm) wide, and 5½ inches (14 cm) deep. If the tray is

1 A food dish made of glazed earthenware and an automatic food dispenser.

10

shallower, the litter is likely to fly all over the room when the rabbit scratches in it. If you plan to keep two animals in the same cage, buy a larger model.

Cage top: A top made of wire grating is best, because a rabbit wants to keep in contact with its environment through its senses of hearing and smell. All cage tops are removable, and many models have a top that flips up, while others have a little door on one side.

Inadvisable: A cage with a top made of plastic. The plastic hood does protect the animal from drafts, but it also isolates your pet from its environment. Moreover, the temperature inside easily can climb too high for the rabbit; excessive heat can harm your pet.

Proper Accessories
Choose equipment of high quality; it will last longer and is easier to maintain.

Food Dishes (Drawing 1)
I recommend a food dish made of glazed earthenware, preferably with a lip that curves inward, designed to keep the food from being pawed out. Plastic bowls are too light; rabbits knock them over and gnaw on them, which can be detrimental to their health.

In addition, hang an automatic dry food dispenser, or hopper, on the wire cage side. It will keep the food from being contaminated by feces and urine.

Hayrack (Drawing 2)
Almost all styles of cages come with a hayrack, or crib, as part of the standard equipment. If

2 A hayrack belongs in every dwarf rabbit's cage.

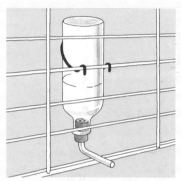

3 In an automatic water dispenser, drinking water will stay clean.

your cage has no hayrack, by all means purchase one (see "The Staple Food: Hay," page 26).

Automatic Water Dispenser (Drawing 3)
Gravity-fed water bottles (automatic water dispensers) have proved reliable. When you buy one of these, ask for a model with a ball-bearing mechanism; the others usually drip constantly. Do not use bowls; the water in them gets dirty quickly.

What Else the Rabbit Needs
Rabbits like to lie on soft bedding, and they also enjoy hav-

ing a little sleeping box. You should provide such a bed if possible.

Bedding (Litter): Litter made especially for small animals, consisting of pine or aspen pressed chips or shavings (available in pet stores) is quite suitable. Ideal for your rabbit: straw (available in pet stores and from farmers).

Sleeping box: A small wooden box measuring about 14 by 14 by 12 inches (35 × 35 × 30 cm), with a lid that can be raised and a round entry hole, will give the rabbit a sense of security and safety. Buy one ready-made from a store that sells breeders' supplies, or build one yourself (see drawing, page 42). It also can serve as a nest box where the doe can kindle (give birth to) her litter.

Litter box: During the rabbit's daily run indoors or on the terrace, it will need a litter box. Litter boxes for cats work quite well (minimum dimensions: 10 by 14 by 5½ inches (25 × 35 × 14 cm)). You can use cat litter, which is highly absorbent.

An Outdoor Pen
During the warm months of the year, your yard is an ideal place for a dwarf rabbit. If you cannot keep an eye on your pet at all times or want to leave it unsupervised, build a stationary outdoor pen.

Minimum size: About 6½ × 6½ feet (2 × 2 m); this will accommodate two or three rabbits.

Safety: Bury the wire mesh at least 12 inches (30 cm) deep in the ground; otherwise, the rabbit will dig its way out underneath. Also, stretch wire mesh over the top of the pen, to keep stray cats from jumping in.

Protection from sun and rain: Cover part of the pen with a roof. The rabbit can move underneath for shelter from blazing sun or rain.

Sleeping box: If you have even a little carpentry skill, you easily can build one yourself, using waterproof sheets of natural wood about ¾ inch (20 mm) thick. The dimensions: 14 by 14 by 12 inches (35 × 35 × 30 cm). Cut the side walls to slant upward toward the back of the box. Let the roof extend about 6 inches (15 cm) beyond the walls, and cover it with tar paper. The roof should be removable or attached with hinges so that you can raise it to take out the old straw. To protect your pet from drafts, saw the entry hole about 4 inches (10 cm) above the bottom of the box. As a safeguard against dampness, set the sleeping box on squared lengths of wood to keep it off the ground. The entry hole should face south. Never place it on the windward side!

Caution: Do not use sheets of plywood or fiberboard, because they contain toxic substances.

5 *Reinforce the frame to make it stable; attach hooks and eyes.*

4 *A movable outdoor pen for spending a few hours in the yard. A spot under a shady tree is an ideal location.*

Russian.

Black Silver.

It is difficult to choose among so many beautiful pure-bred rabbits. Each one has characteristics specific to its breed, set forth in the so-called breed standard. The coat color of the colored dwarfs is precisely the same as that of the larger breeds of the color in question. The term "varieties of markings" is used for dwarf rabbits that have various marks, or patterns, and are not solid-colored.

Gray.

Havana.

Blue-eyed White.

Thuringer.

Black-and-white Lop, broken-colored.

Hotot.

Black.

Blue-and-tan.

Siamese.

White-tipped Black.

Living with a Dwarf Rabbit

Getting the New Arrival Settled

Bring your newly acquired dwarf rabbit home immediately and put it in its cage, which should be equipped with the following:
- A thick layer of bedding with newspapers placed underneath.
- Lukewarm water in an automatic water dispenser.
- Fresh hay in the rack.
- Some food: coarse oats, a commercial feed mixture, a quarter of an apple, and some parsley in your pet's food dish.

How to pick up a dwarf rabbit: Firmly and securely, take hold of the skin between the rabbit's shoulder blades and pick the animal up, while supporting its rear end with your other hand.

- Don't forget: The little sleeping box, so that the rabbit has a place to which it can retreat.

Now leave the animal alone; let it explore and sniff everything in peace and quiet. After all, it has been plucked from surroundings familiar to it and needs time to get acquainted with its new home. If you have children, explain to them why they cannot pick up their new housemate at once and cuddle it. If there are other pets in your household, keep them away from the rabbit. You will have to get the animals accustomed to one another gradually (see page 24).

Once the dwarf rabbit starts to eat and drink (it may even clean itself afterward), the initial shock has been weathered. Now you can put your pet on your lap from time to time, pet it, and talk to it. This will help the rabbit get used to you and the rest of your family. Dwarf rabbits need this kind of physical contact. Each one has its own favorite spot where it likes to be scratched.

Making Friends: Children and Rabbits

You imagined it would be so wonderful: for Easter, you would give your child a real live bunny. And how disappointed you and your child were if the experience turned out to be not so enjoyable after all. Often such problems arise because humans and animals have very different wants. You as parents are now faced with the need to mediate between the child's wishes and the requirements of the dwarf rabbit.

Children want to pet the animal, carry it around with them wherever they go, play with it, and have it constantly available.

Dwarf rabbits need contact, physical closeness, and warmth, so they like to be petted. On the other hand, they also need periods during which they are left in peace and their freedom of movement is not inhibited. Moreover, they are not able to participate in every kind of game your child may want them to. Here you as parents will need to intervene.

Gently explain to your child that a rabbit strongly dislikes being disturbed at mealtime or being taken out of its cage when it wants to rest or sleep. Tell your child that dwarf rabbits need to run around outside the cage at least one hour a day and that they like to play, but—unlike dogs—do not want to run after a ball and will not come when you whistle. Rabbits may perhaps hop on a child's lap to be petted or push against a hand (see "How To: Body Language," page 54).

Tell your child that candy and chocolate are not suitable foods for dwarf rabbits. These animals can tolerate music only if it is not loud, and they greatly dislike being wedged under a child's arm and carried around like a stuffed toy.

Remain firm and teach your child to accept partial responsibility for feeding, cleaning the cage, grooming the rabbit, and performing other small chores in the care of the new pet. This way your child can learn an important lesson in life: Love of a living creature means having time for it, being there when it needs you, and taking responsibility for it.

How to carry a dwarf rabbit: Lay one hand on its neck so that you can act quickly if the dwarf rabbit struggles or tries to jump down.

Picking Up and Carrying Your Pet Properly

People often lift and carry dwarf rabbits the wrong way, and accidents can occur easily.

The right way (see drawings, page 14 and above): With your right hand, get a good, secure hold on the skin of the rabbit's back between its shoulder blades and lift the animal up, while supporting it with your left hand. Now put the rabbit on your arm and hold it there, keeping one hand gently on its neck. This way, you will be able to intervene any time it tries to jump down. Children, too, should learn how to hold the rabbit in order to avoid unfortunate accidents.

The wrong way: Wedging the animal under your arm. The rabbit may start to struggle, and you may even crush its ribs and intestines with this grip. Then it can slip from your arm, fall to the floor, and injure itself—unfortunately, a frequent occurrence.

Important: Pulling it up by the ears is cruel to the animal.

First the rabbit sniffs . . .

. . . then it scrapes vigorously with its paws

In the photos:
During the rabbit's daily run indoors or on the terrace, it needs a litter box. If you fail to provide one, the animal will seek out its own spots in which to relieve itself. In any event, perseverance and patience on your part are necessary until the rabbit is in the habit of using its box.

How Do You Housebreak a Dwarf Rabbit?

Rabbits are extremely clean animals. In their burrows, wild rabbits always leave their droppings in the same spot. Similarly, tame rabbits do not "do their business" randomly all over the cage. Take advantage of this innate sense of cleanliness; while your dwarf rabbit is getting its exercise outside the cage, in your house or on the terrace, get it used to a certain spot—a litter box. I cannot guarantee that the following suggestions will work for you, because success in housebreaking a rabbit depends on the individual animal. Not all my dwarf rabbits are housebroken. At first I was less than delighted about this, but now I simply vacuum up the few pellets that may miss the box without grumbling about it. Don't be discouraged, however. It has been my experience that there are more ways than one to housebreak a rabbit. Here are some sug-

gestions that have proved successful in many instances.

What You Can Do
• When the rabbit leaves its cage for the first time, put a litter box filled with cat litter in the room and place a few pellets of excrement in it.

   Tip: A litter box for dwarf rabbits should have fairly low sides so that they can jump in and out easily.
• Put the dwarf rabbit in the box. Don't despair if it hops out again and relieves itself on the carpet.
• Put the litter box in your pet's favorite corner—for example, in the gap between the end of a cabinet or bookcase and the wall.
• Keep putting the animal in the box, and clean up puddles on the floor or the carpet with a solution of water and vinegar. This will disinfect the spot, and the odor also will offend the rabbit's sensitive nose. Incidentally, the droppings are almost odorless and can be vacuumed up easily when they are dry.

What Else You Can Do

Tip 1: Instead of letting the rabbit out once a day for an hour, try letting it out several times for about 20 minutes each time. Rabbits prefer to exercise frequently for short periods, and they will be more likely to leave their droppings in the cage after their run, rather than all over the room.

Tip 2: If possible, let the rabbit out before you feed it. The urge to relieve itself will be less strong. When you put your pet back in its cage, give it something to eat right away; then it will not interpret being caught and returned to the cage as "punishment."

Important: Never yell at your dwarf rabbit or spank it, even very gently. Doing so may upset the animal and make the process of housebreaking it more difficult.

Now the rabbit "does its business" quickly.

The Daily Run Indoors

If you ever have observed wild rabbits in nature, you know how busily they hop about, cut capers, double back, and disappear with the speed of lightning into a hiding place. Indoor rabbits—although forced to spend most of their time sitting quietly in a cage—exhibit the same behavior. Exercise benefits their sensory perceptions and personality development; strengthens their heart, lungs, and muscles; improves their health; and lengthens their lives. Let your dwarf rabbit run free indoors every day, for as long a time as possible—at least 20 minutes three times a day, or twice a day for correspondingly longer periods.

Without sufficient exercise, rabbits quickly become overweight. Fat animals usually suffer from serious heart and circulatory problems, which frequently prove fatal.

Tip: The first time, keep the dwarf rabbit in one room for its outing. When it feels thoroughly at ease there, the outings can take place in other rooms, the terrace, or the yard. Otherwise,

the animal may feel overtaxed and become insecure and timid.

When the Rabbit is Roaming Free Indoors, Keep This in Mind:

- There should be no valuable carpets and furniture in the room. The rabbit could soil them or chew on them; the latter activity could be harmful to the animal's health.
- The room should not have a smooth floor of parquet or synthetic material, because the rabbit can slip on such a surface. On a stone floor, it could catch cold. If no appropriate floor is available, it is a good idea to build an indoor run (see page 18).
- Electrical cords should be kept out of your pet's reach. Rabbits chew on them, and this could prove fatal. Telephone cords, too, are extremely attractive to rabbits; a dwarf rabbit can gnaw through them in an instant. Keep an eye on your pet, or sheathe the cord in a protective covering (cable armor does the job well).

- Always keep the litter box in the room with the rabbit.
- Open and close doors slowly so that the rabbit does not get caught.
- Be careful when walking around; rabbits often will jump between your feet.

Indoor Runs

If you do not have an appropriate room to allow your rabbit to run, you will need to build an indoor run for it. A child's wooden folding playpen is inexpensive and quite practical.

Stretch fine wire mesh around the playpen. Line the bottom with a sheet of waterproof plastic, and place a rice straw mat on top of it. These natural-fiber mats, available in many department stores, are quite inexpensive and do not slide around. They are wonderful for your rabbit to hop around on or to scratch and scrape on. Your pet can even nibble on a mat without harming itself. Remember: Put the litter box inside the run.

Play Corner for an Indoor Rabbit

Rabbits love holes, hiding places such as hedges and bushes, and the cover provided by tall grass and shrubs. A bare floor where all your pet can do is hop back and forth is downright boring for the animal. Dwarf rabbits that live exclusively indoors—for example, in homes where no terrace or yard is available to them—may spend all their time dozing, even when they are offered ample opportunity to roam free in the house.

To avoid such a situation, my children came up with ideas for making our dwarf rabbits' play corner more interesting. They got large and small cardboard boxes at the supermarket, cut windows and doors in them, and set them up in the rabbits' play area. From then on the animals became increasingly lively. They hopped enthusiastically through the "landscape," jumped on top of the boxes, and played hide-and-seek. Watching and observing the rabbits became far more enjoyable.

Establishing a relationship by sniffing. When two dwarf rabbits meet for the first time, they start out by sniffing each other thoroughly to determine whether they are compatible.

A Home on the Terrace

From spring to early fall, my dwarf rabbits live on the terrace, where they are allowed to run free. Keep the following points in mind when setting up quarters for your rabbit on a terrace:

The floor: Many terrace floors are made of concrete. Your rabbit will very likely catch cold on such a surface, so you will need to put down rice straw mats (see "Indoor Runs," page 18).

Safety: There is a possibility that the rabbit will eventually squeeze through the bars of the terrace or underneath the balustrade, if it does not extend all the way to the floor, and plunge to the ground below. For your rabbit's safety, terraces with bars should be surrounded with a safety wall of wire mesh at least 32 inches (80 cm) high and firmly attached to the floor. If your terrace has a balustrade that is open only at the bottom, you can use wooden planks to cover the open portion.

Tip: Even if your terrace has bars that reach to the floor, attach a board at the bottom. It will protect the rabbit from drafts, and will give your pet something to gnaw on.

Stray cats: If your terrace is at ground level and easily accessible to stray cats or to martens, your dwarf rabbit is in great danger. Put your pet in its cage, securely closed, whenever the animal is to be left unsupervised.

Sun: If sunlight shines on the entire terrace, you will have to create a shady spot where the rabbit can take shelter; otherwise, your pet may suffer a heatstroke. A wooden panel, an awning, or a piece of canvas—which also protects the rabbit from rain—will do the job.

To spend the night outdoors, the rabbit will need a small house for sleeping (see "How To: Setting up the Cage," page 10).

Temperature changes: Get your rabbit used to outdoor temperatures gradually. During times of the year when days are warm and nights cool, put the animal outdoors for a few hours at a time, but bring it back indoors for the night. Once it is warm enough (68°F [20°C]), the rabbit can stay outside day and night.

Remember these too: A food dish and a water dish made of earthenware; a litter box filled with cat litter; a wooden box filled with sand or loose dirt for the rabbit to dig in.

Exercise in the Yard

The ideal place for a dwarf rabbit is, of course, the yard. Let your pet hop around there as much as possible, but stay close by in case it runs away or is chased by dogs or cats. If you want to leave the rabbit unsupervised, you will have to put it in an outdoor run. The How To section on page 10 gives detailed instructions for building such a run yourself.

An Outing in the Country

If you have no yard, occasional outings in the country will do your dwarf rabbit good. Set aside plenty of time for such trips, and keep the following in mind:

• Avoid grassy areas in parks where dogs run free. Your dwarf rabbit can fall prey to a disease by eating plants on which dogs have urinated. In addition, a dog not on its leash might chase and injure the rabbit.

• Country meadows are a better choice, especially if you have a clear view of them. During the hot months of the year, the rabbit will most likely want to have a tree nearby for shade.

It is impossible to "walk" your dwarf rabbit. Unlike a dog, it will not trot along obediently behind you.

A Rabbit on a Leash?

The first few times you take your dwarf rabbit on an outing to the coun-

Dwarf rabbits should never suffer from lack of exercise and boredom, which make them phlegmatic and even ill. Make sure your pet has ample opportunity to run free indoors, on the terrace, or in the yard. Provide some diversion as well—by creating a play corner with caves made of cardboard boxes, for example.

A trip to the country with your children and pet rabbit will be enjoyable if you allow plenty of time for the outing and remember that rabbits, unlike dogs, cannot be taken for walks. These little hoppers need time to get used to the new, exciting surroundings. Keep a close eye on your pet to keep it from being harmed—for example, by dogs running unleashed outdoors.

try, use a rabbit leash. The excitement of the new environment could frighten the animal into running off on its own, and you might not get it back very quickly: just try to catch a high-spirited dwarf rabbit. Later on, you can let the rabbit walk freely, but you should always have the leash along. If a dog should suddenly appear on the scene, for example, you can use the leash to ensure your rabbit's safety.

As a rabbit leash, try the cat harnesses made of soft suede that are available in many pet stores.

Holding the leash properly requires a great deal of sensitivity. Unlike a dog, a rabbit cannot be led along nicely on a leash. A lively rabbit weighing two or three pounds and delicately built cannot be compelled to do anything by force. Parents should make this clear to their children. Younger children, in particular, are often too impatient; they may tug and pull the rabbit in the direction they want it to walk. However, dwarf rabbits do not walk; they hop, jump, and double back. They like to disappear in bushes where you may be unable to follow, and they may stay there for quite some time. The best solution is to wait patiently and try verbally coaxing the rabbit. Under no circumstances should you pull hard or yank at the leash. Preferably, keep your rabbit from hiding in the bushes in the first place. If you approach an area with bushes, pick up your pet carefully and set it down again in an open area.

Vacation Care

A dwarf rabbit that is provided with enough food and water can be left at home alone for as long as one or two days. If you plan to be gone for much longer, there are several possible solutions.

Take it along: Short car journeys, a destination in a moderate climate, a fixed location with an opportunity for outings (a vacation house, for example).

Leave it at home: Looked after by someone who has experience with rabbits. Make sure to arrange for exercise periods, especially if you have only one rabbit. And remind the caretaker to pet the rabbit daily.

Board it elsewhere: In a pet store, if it is allowed to run at least once a day and if the cage is not next to animals that may be bothersome to the rabbit—loudly singing birds, for example.

Another suggestion: Let someone "foster" the rabbit during your vacation. Many animal-welfare organizations provide addresses of people who are willing to keep pets for short periods in exchange for a small fee.

Tip: If you will be traveling abroad, contact the appropriate consulate ahead of time to find out what documents are required for traveling with your pet. Get a health certificate from the veterinarian.

Not advisable and to be resorted to only in an emergency: Leaving your pet in an animal shelter or with a breeder, where the rabbit will have to sit alone in a hutch all day.

Two who like to cuddle.
Dwarf rabbits enjoy being petted if they are in the mood. However, children have to learn the right way to pick up and carry a rabbit; otherwise, unfortunate accidents may occur.

Rabbits are clean animals. They wash themselves, including their ears, with great care. The coat is always smooth and silky, unless the animal is sick. Apart from feeding and cleaning the cage regularly, a rabbit that is properly kept needs little care.

Clipping the Claws
(Drawings 1 and 2)

If your rabbit has little opportunity to wear down its claws naturally, by scraping, they will curve inward as they grow and hamper the animal's movements. Consequently, the nails should be clipped. Ideally, because trimming the claws is a delicate procedure, have an expert (a veterinarian or a breeder) teach you the necessary maneuvers first. Follow these guidelines carefully:
• Work with a helper. One person can hold and pet the rabbit

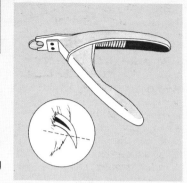

2 Special clippers for cutting claws; the correct way to angle the cut.

while the other does the trimming.
• When cutting a claw, hold the rabbit's paw gently but firmly and push the fur covering the claw slightly to the side.
   Pointer: Each forepaw has five claws, one of which grows to the side; the rear paws have four claws apiece.
• Try not to splinter the horny substance of the claw. Use special clippers (see Drawing 2) for cutting the rabbit's nails. These tools are available in pet stores.

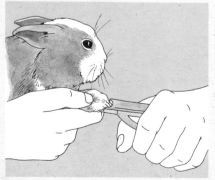

1 Have someone help you cut your pet's claws. One person can hold the rabbit and stroke it while the other wields the clippers.

• Be careful not to injure the blood vessels that are located inside the claws along with nerve endings. Cutting into this portion of the nail hurts the rabbit and causes bleeding. The best method is to hold the claws in front of a light, such as a flashlight. This way, you will be able to see the blood vessels more easily.
• To be on the safe side, don't cut the nails back too far.
   Tip: Always give your rabbit plenty of opportunities to use its claws for scratching and scraping. Indoors or on a terrace, provide a rice straw mat for this purpose (see page 18).

Grooming
(Drawing 3)

Rabbits keep their fur clean themselves. However, during molting your dwarf rabbit will require daily brushing. Do this with a brush that is not overly hard. Once in a while, try brushing against the lay of the fur. Many rabbits enjoy being brushed regularly in and out of molting season, because it stimulates their blood circulation.

   Important: Do not bathe your dwarf rabbit or give it a shower.

   Genital area: Occasionally a discharge with a sweetish smell collects in the genital area of the rabbit (right and left of the sexual orifice). Remove it carefully, using a cotton pad with a few drops of oil.

   Checking the teeth (Drawings 4 and 5): A rabbit's teeth, like its claws, grow continually. To keep them at their proper length, the animal needs something to gnaw on, such as hard bread or twigs (see "Something to Nibble," page 28). Hay should be made available for your pet at all times.

Overly long teeth will get in your pet's way when it tries to eat, and should be ground down by a veterinarian. Try to avoid the need for this procedure, which is highly unpleasant for the rabbit.

Pointer: If there is a malocclusion, a hereditary abnormality, in your pet's bite, you will have no choice but to have its teeth ground down by a veterinarian at regular intervals.

Cleaning the Cage and Accessories

Regular, thorough cleaning of the cage and accessories is an important part of looking after a pet rabbit. Do not neglect the cleaning chores.

3 To groom the rabbit's coat, use a brush that is not overly hard.

Every day, clean the water dispenser and food dishes:
• Wash out the containers with very warm, clear water.
• Wash the water bottle with clean water and a bottle brush reserved exclusively for this purpose.
• Fill the water bottle with lukewarm water. Never use ice-cold water, which can disturb the rabbit's digestion.

Twice a week, clean the cage, following these guidelines:
• If the cage is fairly clean, wipe out the plastic tray at the bottom with a wet cloth.
• If it is dirty, scrub the tray with hot (but not too hot) water and a mild household cleanser. Then wipe it completely dry and put in fresh litter.

Tip: If you lay newspaper under the litter, the tray will be easier to clean. Make sure, however, that your rabbit does not nibble on or eat the paper, because the printer's ink contains additives that will likely harm the animal. If your pet does show a fondness for newspaper, you will have to use paper grocery bags.

Once a month, put the wire cage top in your bathtub or other suitable vessel and wash it under a warm shower. Use this method more often, of course, if necessary.

Disinfecting the cage is necessary only if the rabbit is ill, or once a year as a preventive measure. Ask your veterinarian or pet store dealer to recommend a disinfectant that is safe for rabbits.

4 The rabbit's teeth should meet as shown above.

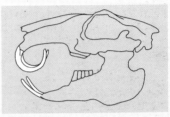

5 Your rabbit's teeth should not look like this.

Tip: If you have a garden, add the rabbit droppings and straw from your pet's cage to the compost heap. Rabbit manure contains primarily nitrogen, potassic acid, and phosphoric acid, along with calcium. Earthworms will grow well in the compost, and it will decay extremely well.

23

Dwarf Rabbits and Other Pets

Many people who are fond of animals as pets have more than one type of pet. If a dwarf rabbit is introduced into such a household, the following information is important:
- Dwarf rabbits and guinea pigs: They get along well and can even be kept together in a cage of the right size.
- Birds: Rabbits have sensitive ears. If your birds sing or squawk loudly, keep the rabbit in another room.
- Dogs and cats: They will not immediately make friends with their new housemate. Because of their hunting instincts, they may regard the dwarf rabbit as prey. Cats of any breed will antagonize a dwarf rabbit. With dogs, however, breed plays a role. For example, a hunting dog will have more difficulty adjusting to a rabbit than a watchdog. If the animals grow up together, the adjustment period is likely to be smooth. Even older animals, however, can learn—with your help—to respect each other.

Getting Used to Other Pets

Close friendships can develop among different types of pets, but sometimes efforts to promote a good relationship will be futile. If this is the case, you will have to keep the animals separate. There are no generally applicable rules, because dwarf rabbits vary greatly in their reaction to other animals. My three rabbits, for example, were successful in quite different ways where our playful, high-spirited male cat was concerned. Mohrle, the youngest rabbit, deliberately avoided any sort of tussling. Trixi, the second-oldest rabbit, is curious and playful herself. She sometimes participated in the cat's games, but also defended herself if the cat became too boisterous. Mümmi, the "boss," would tolerate no rival of any kind. At first, every

time the cat made an approach, she cuffed him vigorously. In time, the cat began to flee as soon as she dashed toward him.

To get your new dwarf rabbit acquainted with a pet that is already part of the household, follow the three steps outlined below. Do not begin these procedures, however, until the rabbit has settled in and is familiar with its new environment.

Exercises for Dogs and Rabbits

1. Bring the dog on a leash to the rabbit's cage. Speak soothingly, pet the dog, and praise it if its behavior is friendly. If it barks, reprimand it with a "Phooey!" and pull sharply on the leash.

2. Put the dwarf rabbit on your lap. It will be at or above the dog's eye level, so the dog cannot dominate it. Sniffing and licking between the animals are permissible, and you also can let the dog smell your hand. If the dog behaves aggressively, scold it and give the leash a vigorous tug. Otherwise, praise and pet both animals.

3. When the animals are used to each other, let the dwarf rabbit run free in the room. Holding the dog's collar, lead it up to the rabbit, speak soothingly, pet it, and let go of the collar if its behavior is friendly. Do not let the dog chase the rabbit; this could frighten the smaller animal.

Exercises for Cats and Rabbits

1. Let the cat go up to the cage. Pet it and speak affectionately to it. If it puts a paw into the cage, reprimand it, but do not yell or get panicky. If it still does not remove the paw, sprinkle a little water on the cat.

2. Put the rabbit, then the cat, on your lap and pet them. Let each animal smell your hands to get acquainted with the new odor.

3. When the animals are getting along, let the rabbit run free in the

Close friendships sometimes do develop between dwarf rabbits and other household pets, but you cannot take this for granted. With dogs and cats in particular, it is important to let the animals get used to each other slowly, one step at a time. If this doesn't work, you will have to keep the animals at a distance from each other.

The rabbit stretches itself out luxuriously on the dug-up soil.

room, but put the cat on a leash for a while. This exercise is difficult, because a hopping rabbit appeals strongly to a cat's hunting and play instincts. Do not let the cat loose until it no longer tries to chase the rabbit.

Getting Acquainted with Other Rabbits

Rabbits enjoy living with other members of their species. Nevertheless, proceed carefully when you want a second dwarf rabbit to join one already in your care.

1. In the beginning, arrange the two cages side by side so that the rabbits can see and sniff each other. Later, leave one animal in its cage while the other roams free. If the latter marks its territory and leaves droppings around the room, its behavior is normal. Do not intervene!

2. Take both rabbits on your lap, pet them, and let them sniff each other. Hold the dominant animal firmly but gently, so that it does not try to bite the other.

3. When the animals are used to each other, let them run free in a neutral room that the already-established rabbit does not regard as its territory, with ample space for them to stay out of each other's way. If serious biting incidents occur, put the dominant rabbit somewhere else. After fighting to establish their hierarchy, my rabbits got along well.

Nutrition

All dwarf rabbits need greens and succulent foods. Some examples of suitable foods are kohlrabi, carrots, cauliflower, dandelions, apples, and parsley.

What Dwarf Rabbits Like to Eat

Nature sets a richly laden table for wild rabbits. They eat plants of all kinds, buds, leaves, and bark, and they supplement these foods with berries, other fruits, mushrooms, and occasionally even a small bug. With the variety of this diet, wild rabbits rarely suffer from any nutritional deficiencies. Moreover, in nature the change in diet that accompanies the slow changing of the seasons is always gradual. Thus the rabbit's sensitive gastrointestinal system is never overtaxed by a sudden switch to another kind of food.

Similarly, in feeding your dwarf rabbit, you should avoid a sudden change in diet and make sure you are providing a variety of nutritious foods. You will find suggestions for a feeding plan on page 30. Most rabbits are little gourmets, and every animal develops its own definite food preferences. My dwarf rabbit Mümmi, for example, liked to eat a strawberry now and then; Mohrle preferred parsley; and Trixi would pounce with delight on pale leaves of Belgian endive.

The Staple Food: Hay

Your dwarf rabbit needs hay every day year round, summer and winter. This roughage aids digestion and provides calcium and magnesium along with the essential bulk. Put enough in the hayrack to last your pet until the next day. Pet stores sell hay packaged in small bags. You can also buy large sacks or bales of hay from a farmer.

When Buying Hay, Keep This in Mind:

• High-grade hay contains cuttings of young grasses, clover, and herbs. It smells fragrant and looks slightly greenish.

• Rowen is the season's second crop of hay, also known as the aftermath. Because it is especially tender, it is suitable for rabbits that need a bland diet.

• Low-grade hay and old hay lack the valuable herbs. In addition, old hay is extremely dusty, and the dust affects rabbits' respiratory passages and causes sneezing. Do not buy yellowish hay either: it consists of dried-out, lignified grasses that are not easily digestible for rabbits.

Warning: Do not feed your pet hay that has not been dried; it will cause colic.

Commercial Feeds

Most pet stores and the pet sections of large department stores sell packaged feed for dwarf rabbits. This feed contains kernels and flakes of various kinds of grains, small seeds, and pellets of a greenish or brownish color. The pellets are composed of pressed hay enriched with vitamins and minerals. Because hay is a major nutritional requirement, make sure such pellets are present in whatever commercial feed mixture you buy. However, I observed that my own dwarf rabbits regularly left the pellets uneaten in the food dish. The little gourmets simply do not care for processed food; they prefer hay still redolent of fresh grasses. However, other rabbits eat the pellets with undisguised eagerness.

Unfortunately, some commercial feeds contain grain kernels that have not been sufficiently crushed and mashed. Consequently, I recommend adding a tablespoonful of coarsely ground cereal grains (oats, millet, wheat) to the mixture. Your dwarf rabbit will enjoy the flakes, which it can digest and utilize better than unprocessed kernels.

Tip: I advise against experimenting with homemade mixtures. To put together a successful mix, you need detailed information about rabbits' nutritional needs. Otherwise, your pet will show symptoms of dietary deficiencies.

Greens and Succulent Foods

Greens and succulent (juicy or moist) foods are the most healthful foods for dwarf rabbits. Fodder plants, vegetables, and fruits are highly nutritious and rich in protein and calcium. Do not be misled by claims that these foods make rabbits fat and sick. If you feed your pet properly (see "Ten Rules for Feeding," page 29), greens and succulent foods will provide the animal appropriate nourishment.

Highly suitable fodder plants you can gather: dandelion greens, ribwort and other similar plantains, milfoil, comfrey, common mugwort, goosefoot, orach, hare's-tail grass, alfalfa, yellow clover, and young nettles. Collect only plants that you recognize!

Less suitable is red clover, which causes flatulence. Mix very small quantities of it with other greens, and do not pick it before it blooms.

Poisonous are autumn crocus (*Colchicum autumnale*), fool's parsley, hemlock, deadly nightshade, black nightshade, laburnum, and members of the yew family. Never assume that your dwarf rabbit will know instinctively to avoid these plants. Do not feed them to your pet under any circumstances!

Highly suitable foods from your kitchen and garden: carrots, carrot tops, lamb's lettuce, Belgian endive, chicory, radish leaves, celery stalks, celery root or celeriac, kohlrabi, kohlrabi leaves, fennel, green herbage, leaves from pea vines, sunflowers, Jerusalem artichokes, apples, and pears. In summer, you can occasionally offer the rabbit a strawberry or raspberry. Particularly good for dwarf rabbits are potherbs such as parsley, mustard leaves, sage, caraway, borage, savory, dill, and lovage.

Less suitable: raw potatoes, head lettuce (especially in winter and spring, when the lettuce available has been grown in a hothouse and is full of nitrates), and all varieties of cabbage, which generally cause flatulence. Exceptions are Chinese or

Fruits, vegetables, and other green foods are essential parts of a dwarf rabbit's diet. Without them, your pet may show symptoms of nutritional deficiency.

The doe and her seven-week-old young enjoy a variety of foods.

Napa cabbage, Brussels sprouts, and cauliflower, which the rabbit can eat in small quantities now and then.

Poisonous are potato sprouts and raw beans.

Something to Nibble

Dwarf rabbits should have something to gnaw on so that their teeth, which never stop growing, will be worn down. Old, hard, dry bread, if it is not moldy and has no added spices or salt, is good for this purpose. Do not give your pet too much bread, be-

cause it is high in calories. Once in a while, offer the rabbit crispbread or knäckebrød, a flat, thin, brittle, unleavened rye bread. Most pet stores sell vegetable crackers and similar products, which you also may give your rabbit from time to time.

Your dwarf rabbit also will be delighted if you bring it some twigs with buds and young shoots to nibble from your walk in the woods. Your pet is exceedingly fond of hazelnut, beech, willow, and fir twigs, as well as twigs from fruit trees.

Pointer: Never feed the rabbit frozen twigs or twigs that have been sprayed with pesticides.

Medicinal Herbs

It is important to know that the rabbit, a herbivorous animal, responds extremely well to medicinal herbs as a treatment for both minor and major diseases.

Nettles: These plants are commonly regarded as weeds. Nonetheless, they are rich in calcium, iron, phosphorus, and protein, and the vitamin D they contain builds bones, cleanses the blood, and aids in digestion. Nettles also stimulate milk production in nursing does. Feed your pet fresh plants whole, but let them wilt slightly first, to lessen the stinging effect. In winter, dried nettles also are quite useful as hay. Cut nettles several times during the summer and hang them up in bunches in a shady spot that has good air circulation. Do not let them dry up in the blazing sun, and do not gather any nettles that have lignified, or become woody.

Milfoil: Many people know milfoil as a medicinal tea, or potion, that has an anti-inflammatory and anti-spasmodic effect on the stomach. Give your pet fresh or dried milfoil as a specific for flatulence and intestinal diseases, or mix it with the rabbit's food as a preventive measure.

Jerusalem artichoke: Jerusalem artichokes are extremely valuable, high-yield fodder plants. We humans eat the sweetish, potatolike tuber, but rabbits prefer the young tops, which are rich in protein and easy to digest.

Drinking Water Is Important

Contrary to popular belief, it is not true that rabbits drink almost no water at all. Because they, unlike humans, are unable to perspire, they have to regulate their heat exchange by panting and by increasing their intake of liquids. Succulent foods do not contain enough moisture to satisfy rabbits. Dwarf rabbits must have drinking water, and your pet should be allowed to decide for itself when and how much to drink. Fill the water dispenser half full of fresh water every day, and make sure it is always within easy reach in the rabbit's indoor cage. The water you provide should be at room temperature, about 64 to 68°F (18–20°C).

Pointer: Dwarf rabbits drink a great deal on hot days, in dry, heated rooms, and when they are given dry food almost exclusively. Nursing does and the thick-wooled dwarf Angoras, too, need large amounts of water.

Ten Rules for Feeding

1. Greens and succulent foods should always be fresh when given to your pet. After half an hour, remove any leftovers from the rabbit's cage. The uneaten food could shrivel, ferment, rot, or grow moldy. Spoiled greens can cause severe health problems. Always put hay in the rack at once to keep it from getting dirty on the cage floor.

2. Don't make a sudden change in your rabbit's diet. If you give your pet primarily dry food, don't switch in one day to fresh greens. Rabbits develop gastronintestinal problems in response to abrupt changes in their diet.

3. Wash fruits and vegetables well, shake the water off, and let them drip-dry.

4. Never give the rabbit anything straight from the refrigerator.

5. Never feed your pet frozen, canned, or cooked vegetables.

6. Never gather green foods along the roadside (these may contain lead from automobile exhaust) or in parks where dogs relieve them-

A varied diet and sufficient exercise will keep your dwarf rabbit healthy and vigorous. Overweight rabbits soon develop heart and circulatory problems that frequently prove fatal. Your pet's diet should include hay, commercial dry feed, something to nibble, and suitable greens and succulent foods.

selves (these foods can transmit disease).

7. Always keep the rabbit's diet varied. Give your pet small quantities of food, and include greens with sufficient hay. Variety in the rabbit's diet will prevent digestive problems.

8. Feed at regular intervals; the rabbit's stomach will get used to a routine.

9. Make sure your pet gets enough exercise to stay healthy. If the rabbit puts on weight, institute a weekly fast day on which only water and hay are available. Overweight rabbits can quickly develop fatty degeneration of the heart muscle and die.

10. Gather plants and herbs from meadows and green areas that are not under cultivation, fertilized, or treated with pesticides. Follow the same guidelines in your own yard as well. You will do yourself and your rabbit a favor.

Suggested Feeding Plan, with Amounts and Times

Times	Young Rabbits (up to 3 months old)	Dwarf Rabbits (up to 3⅓ lbs [1.5 kg])
Morning	Commercial feed, ½–¾ oz (15–20 g)	Commercial feed, ¾–1 oz (20–30 g)
Every 2 to 3 days, in addition:	Coarse flakes of wheat, oats, and spelt: 1 tsp	Coarse flakes: 1 T
Afternoon or early evening	⅘ oz (25 g) of easily digestible foods, such as lamb's lettuce, fennel, parsley, Belgian endives; in summer, dandelions, alfalfa	¾–1⅕ oz (20–35 g) of lettuce (but not head lettuce!) or greens or up to 2 oz (60 g) of vegetables—carrots, kohlrabi, celery root, fennel
Daily	Put in the hayrack the amount of hay the animal can eat in a 24-hour period.	Put in the hayrack the amount of hay the animal can eat in a 24-hour period.
Once a week, something to nibble	Old bread, ⅘ oz (25 g). Caution: If the rabbit tends to put on weight, feed it knäckebrød instead.	Old bread, 1–1⅕ oz (30–35 g). Caution: If the rabbit tends to put on weight, feed it knäckebrød instead.
	Twigs and, in fall, dry leaves—any amount	Twigs and, in fall, dry leaves—any amount
Once a week, something to nibble	One quarter of an apple or pear	One quarter of an apple or pear

If Your Dwarf Rabbit Gets Sick

Keeping Your Pet Healthy

Dwarf rabbits are naturally resistant, undemanding, and robust. With the right living conditions and good care, healthy animals with no hereditary handicaps will seldom get sick. To help your pet stay healthy, provide a clean, dry cage in the proper location, pay close attention to the rules for feeding dwarf rabbits, and give the animal ample opportunity to run free and exercise. Remember to give the rabbit the understanding and attention it requires.

In periods of increased stress, your pet's resistance is lower than normal and you will need to give it special care:

• When young rabbits are being switched from doe's milk to solid food.

• When does are pregnant or lactating.

• When there is a sudden change in climate or temperature. Rabbits cannot adjust quickly to such fluctuations.

Important: If an animal does get sick despite all your care, it is not able to tell you how it feels. It is up to you to notice the first symptoms of a possible illness and take some action to help your pet (see pages 34 and 35). Just don't try to play veterinarian!

Initial Symptoms

If you regularly spend time with your dwarf rabbit, you will immediately notice any change in its behavior and appearance (see the checklist on pages 34 and 35). For example, if the rabbit no longer hops friskily to the cage door when you bring it food, but stays listlessly hunched in a corner, with flattened ears, dull eyes, and a fixed stare, chances are something is wrong with it. Does the rabbit's abdomen look caved in or greatly distended? Is its coat rough? Does it keep scratching itself? Is it breathing irregularly or behaving abnormally in some other way? These are the first signs of a potential illness.

First Aid Procedures

Even if your dwarf rabbit seems to be suffering from only mild indisposition or a minor health problem, take action at once. In many cases you can eliminate the causes, and the rabbit will be hopping around again, happy as a lark.

Here are some ways you can restore your rabbit to health if the problem is not serious.

Mild diarrhea (if the rabbit's general state of health is unimpaired): Change the litter in the cage at frequent intervals and keep the rabbit warm. Give it only lukewarm camomile tea and boiled, unsalted rice. If the diarrhea persists for longer than 48 hours, consult your veterinarian.

Mild constipation: Do not give your rabbit any more dry food, but

If you look after your dwarf rabbit properly, bouts of sickness will be rare. The prerequisites for good health are a clean, dry cage in the right location, suitable food, plenty of exercise, understanding, and attention.

First it washes its tiny nose . . .

. . . then it's time for the back.

In the photos:
A shiny, smooth coat is an indicator of good health and well-being. When only two weeks old, bunnies make their first attempts to wash themselves, and soon they have perfected the technique, as the photos of the four-week-old dwarf rabbit above show.

offer it plenty of liquids—caraway tea, for example. Feed it a teaspoonful of olive oil, and make sure it gets plenty of exercise. If no improvement is evident after 24 hours, see your veterinarian at once.

Sniffles caused by irritation: Eliminate the possible causes—for example, dusty hay or caustic cleansers that produce gases. If in doubt, take the animal to the veterinarian.

Emergency treatment for heatstroke: Here you have to act quickly. Put the animal in the shade at once and offer it lukewarm water. Using damp cloths that are cool—never ice-cold—cool the rabbit's head, then its legs. Feed it some black coffee to stimulate its circulation: half a teaspoonful for young rabbits, one teaspoonful for full-grown animals.

The Dwarf Rabbit as a Patient
There scarcely exists a quieter and more patient invalid than the dwarf rabbit. Even when suffering severe pain, it will not cry out, whimper, or whine. Only the look in its eyes will tell you how it feels. Changes in its behavior and appearance are its only way of showing you that it is ill. Pay close attention to these signs so that you can give your veterinarian the appropriate information. Be prepared to answer the following questions when you talk to the veterinarian:
• When did you first notice a change in your rabbit's behavior?
• When, what, and how much did it eat?
• How do its feces look? Does it suffer from diarrhea or constipation?

When taking care of an ill dwarf rabbit, follow these basic guidelines, along with your veterinarian's recommendations:

- Keep the animal in a cage of its own, away from other rabbits—in another room, if possible. Do this as a precaution when you notice the first signs of illness.
- Scrupulously keep everything clean. If the rabbit has a contagious disease, frequently change the litter in its cage and disinfect the cage and its furnishings.

Caution: If your pet is suffering from a contagious disease, ask your veterinarian what disinfectant to use.

- Feed the sick animal a bland diet. With some diseases, the animal will have to fast.
- Make sure the area near the cage is quiet.
- Changes in temperature, drafty air, and other stressful factors are an additional burden on the animal; avoid them at all costs.
- Be patient. Fear and pain may cause the rabbit to bite you. Be understanding; your rabbit needs you now.

Having Your Pet Put to Sleep

If your dwarf rabbit is suffering from a painful, incurable disease, your best course of action may be to have the animal put to sleep. Naturally, your child may be upset by this decision. The way you explain the need to say good-bye to a beloved playmate and discuss the concept of death in general is up to you. Seek the help of your veterinarian in deciding whether to put the animal to sleep.

The death of a pet, even when it occurs naturally, is always emotionally taxing for the animal's owners. We are losing a friend, a family member, one we have come to love deeply over a period of years. My family felt this way about all our rabbits, especially our

The little paws also have to be licked clean.

dwarf Mohrle. She was eight years old when she died and had been with us the longest: we got her as an eight-week-old "baby girl." She brought three litters into the world, sired by three different males, and each time it was a wonderful, exciting event. When her last mate, an Angora named Dicki, had to be put to sleep because of a hereditary paralysis, we could see her wasting away. Two months later she was dead too, of heart failure—a common cause of death among dwarf rabbits, especially at her age. I am convinced, though, that grief over the loss of Dicki was a contributing factor in her death.

Checklist for Possible Health Problems and Diseases

You can give your dwarf rabbit drops with a disposable syringe (without a needle!). Insert it from the side, behind the gnawing teeth. Holding the nape of the rabbit's neck, depress the plunger of the syringe slowly, so that the animal does not choke.

Symptoms	Possible Causes That You Easily Can Remedy Yourself
Feces soft and pasty to watery, may also smell sourish. Belly and anus smeared with feces.	Sudden change in diet (from dry food to greens), spoiled, overly cold food or water, gastrointestinal problems due to damp bedding and drafty air
Stops eating, excretes only tiny hard balls of feces or none at all, despite straining; body slightly bloated	Too little exercise, lack of drinking water, sudden switch from greens to dry food exclusively, attendant symptom of infectious diseases, spoiled food
Slight, clear nasal discharge, occasional sneezing	Irritation caused by gases from caustic cleaning agents, dusty hay, vitamin deficiency, general lowered resistance (some rabbits are allergic to hay!)
Tearing eyes, reddened, perhaps swollen, lids, watery to pus-like discharge	Attendant symptom of colds, irritation from dust or foreign bodies, injury from scratching or biting, overly long fur (in Angoras, for example)
More rapid breathing, body trembles	Buildup of heat in the body caused by direct sun or excessive heat from nearby radiators
Reddened skin, slight fur loss, small bald patch	Molting in spring and fall, allergy, vitamin deficiency, fur torn out by bite from another rabbit
Sits around listlessly, moves about too little	Is lonely, needs companionship, gets too little attention, boredom, no stimulating, interesting place to run (rabbits also grow quieter with age!)

If These Symptoms Are Also Present, There Is Cause for Alarm	Possible Diagnosis and Immediate Treatment by Veterinarian
Refuses to eat, loses strength, sits in cage trembling with fear, grinds teeth from pain, body distended, blood in stool	Poisoning from chemically polluted greens, intestinal infection, and, most commonly, coccidiosis (highly contagious for other rabbits; especially dangerous for young rabbits; take along a stool sample by all means!); isolate the animal
Body severely bloated, grinds teeth from pain, violent drumming with hind legs, shortness of breath, and circulatory insufficiency	Tympanitis (middle-ear infection), see veterinarian at once—can be fatal
Thick, sticky, yellowish nasal discharge, which rabbit tries to remove by snorting and by wiping it off with its paws; chest and front paws smeared; lack of appetite; general listlessness; possibly also coughing	Contagious sniffles (isolate rabbit from other animals at once), onset of pneumonia in addition
Eyes swollen completely shut, gelatinous, pasty swelling on head, nodules, increasing numbers of boils that break open	Myxomatosis, regarded as virtually incurable, vaccination recommended in epidemic areas
Nostrils flared, body violently trembling, mouth may be open, very rapid, shallow breathing	Heatstroke, extremely dangerous; see veterinarian at once, or if not possible, see page 32 for emergency treatment!
Severe fur loss, sticky, crusty coating, frequent scratching, rabbit tilts head and shakes it violently	Mange (infestation by mites), fungi
Doesn't run at all, grinds teeth from pain, tucks its legs under or stretches them out oddly, drags them, loses sense of balance	Broken bone, torn ligament, dislocated joint, internal injury from getting squashed by a door or being dropped, paralysis due to hereditary disease

In the ears, scale formation and a smeary or crusty coating can be signs of mange. Another symptom is frequent tilting and shaking of the head. Take your pet to the veterinarian without delay. If you have several rabbits, isolate the sick one at once; the disease is contagious.

Breeding and Reproduction

It is surely the most natural thing in the world for animals to conceive and bear young. I can well understand if you suddenly announce one day to the rest of your family: "Our dwarf rabbit ought to have some babies." I frequently have encountered this desire in people who want to preserve for their pet some remnant of natural behavior, alienated as the rabbit is from its original habitat.

However, we should remember that we and our pets are not living out in the great world of nature, but indoors in a house with a yard, or even in a tiny apartment. In these surroundings, no natural selection through the food supply, the size of the territory, or enemies can take place. Rabbits are able to reproduce "boundlessly."

You and your children are probably the ones who will derive the most pleasure from a nest full of adorable, frisky little bundles of fur. Although your desire is quite understandable, do not lose sight of the fact that your pleasure should be accompanied by a great deal of responsibility. On the basis of my experience, I would like to ask you to consider several factors before reaching a decision about whether to breed your rabbits.

If You Want Your Dwarf Rabbit to Raise a Litter
• Do you and your family have time to take proper care of the pregnant doe and, later, her offspring?
• Do you have a vacation, a move, or a busy period at work slated for the time of the doe's pregnancy (one month) and the time needed for the

little rabbits to grow up (two months)? If so, it may be better to postpone your nursery duties.
• Is your indoor cage large enough to accommodate the nest box along with the doe and her fidgety offspring?
• If you want to keep one or more of the young, you will have to provide additional housing (another cage, a new hutch).
• If you want to give the young rabbits away later, get the process started early (through relatives, neighbors, classified advertisements in the newspaper). It is not always easy to find really good homes for the bunnies.
• Talk with your children ahead of time about giving up the young rabbits; otherwise, there may be tears later.

Breeding with Purebred Dwarfs
The goal of a good breeder is to produce animals that are not only healthy, but also beautiful. Beautiful, in the case of dwarf rabbits, means that the animal conforms as closely as possible to the ideal concepts defined in the breed standard (see page 45). Many breeders' chief ambition is to exhibit their animals and have them judged. Breeders also keep a stock

A female Thuringer, one and a half years old. These chamois-colored rabbits have a dark mask, dark ears, and dark "boots," all of which blend very gradually into the ground color of the coat.

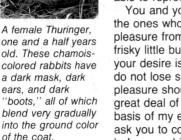

Thuringer Dwarf Lop.
This breed is high-spirited and weighs somewhat more than the other purebred dwarfs. Dwarf Lops may weigh as much as 4 pounds 7 ounces (2 kg), and their drooping ears are 9 to 11 inches (24–28 cm) long.

record book, have their rabbits tattooed, and specialize in a particular color or marking. Often thirty or forty rabbits will be born before one of show quality appears. Obviously, you need detailed knowledge of hereditary transmission and breeds, as well as a great deal of time and space, to pursue such a hobby—an apartment with a terrace is not sufficient. Before attempting to breed rabbits, it is a good idea to join a local rabbit breeders' club. Experienced breeders will be able to give you advice and support, and they can help you obtain the purebred animals you want.

Choosing the Parent Animals

Many inexperienced pet owners are familiar with the following scenario: Believing they had acquired two female siblings, they did not suspect anything immediately when one of the animals became increasingly plump. Because rabbits also give birth, or kindle, quietly and unobtrusively (see page 40), the owners were absolutely flabbergasted one morning to see four adorable little dwarfs tumbling along behind the big animals. All you really can do then is make the best of it, enjoy the new family, and take good care of them. As a rule, however, we should try to plan parenthood for dwarf rabbits.

• Both parent animals must be in good health. They should not be molting at the time of mating; this would be too stressful for them.

• Age is an important factor. Although dwarf rabbits reach sexual maturity at 12 weeks, they should not be bred until later. Does that are mated too soon may suffer permanent physical damage. The minimum age for a first mating is eight months for does, seven months for bucks.

Pointer: Upon reaching sexual maturity (after the twelfth week of life),

does and bucks should be housed separately.

• The buck should be the same size or, preferably, somewhat smaller than the doe, never the other way around. Otherwise, the young will be too large and complications may occur during the birth.

• Pay close attention to the breed characteristics of dwarf rabbits (see page 7). Rabbits of different colors can be mixed with each other, but many "colorful" surprises will be the result. The offspring will stay small, but they no longer will be purebred animals.

For breeding according to standard (see page 45), only purebred dwarf rabbits are used: registered, tattooed animals of the same breed.

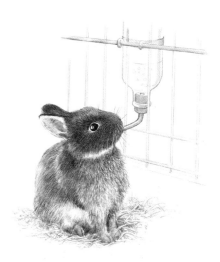

Drinking water stays clean in this gravity-fed watering system. Dwarf rabbits, particularly lactating does, should have fresh water available at all times.

Heat

Dwarf rabbits, unlike other household pets, are able to conceive almost all year round. Often, a change in diet (oats are said to be a stimulant) or room temperature is enough to trigger a dwarf rabbit's readiness to mate. Even the mere presence of a male rabbit in a doe's vicinity can send her into heat.

On occasion, the proximity of a male will induce a false pregnancy. The doe gathers straw, carries it in her mouth into the nest box, and spends her time excitedly scratching around in the litter. Don't let yourself be deceived by this behavior. The only sure signs of a genuine pregnancy are a rounded abdomen and swollen mammary glands. In addition, shortly before a pregnant doe is due to kindle, she will begin to pluck fur from her abdomen to use in lining her nest.

Courtship and Mating

For the animals, the most natural time to come together for mating is the period when they are allowed to run free. Stiff-legged, the buck will circle around the doe and lick her head and neck. These actions, along with the buck's scent, induce in her a readiness to mate. She drops her initial reticence, begins to caress the buck, then acts as if she is going to run away and waits for him to hop after her.

The actual mating usually occurs very rapidly; it lasts no more than 15 seconds. During mating, the buck mounts the doe's back, while she raises her pelvis toward him in a receptive attitude. After ejaculating, the buck slides to the doe's side with a short growl and lies there for a few seconds, exhausted. I often have seen a buck circle the reclining doe a few more times, then lie down beside her and lick her affectionately.

In most cases, a single mating is sufficient, although wild rabbits usually mate several times.

Pointer: If you want the animals to mate in a cage, always put the doe in the buck's cage. In the doe's cage, she would defend her territory and her biting might injure the male badly. Moreover, the buck first would want to mark his new surroundings and thus would not fulfill his real assignment. In his own cage, however, the buck feels secure and is not perturbed by attacks. Occasionally, a doe refuses to be serviced by a certain buck. Be understanding of her feelings, and try again with another animal.

The Pregnant Doe

Gestation length in rabbits is determined by a birth hormone. In dwarf rabbits, the gestation period usually lasts 28 to 31 days. In the case of very small litters, it may extend to 33 days. Treat the doe with special consideration at this time, and be prepared for changes in her behavior.

You will be able to see changes in the doe's behavior during the four weeks following the mating. Animals that previously were calm and peaceable may become nervous and even bite and scratch. Does that were nervous and fidgety, however, usually become quite peaceable at this time and seem almost phlegmatic. Six days after mating, all does follow a basic instinct: they scratch around in their litter, rummage through everything, and try to make a burrow. Be sure to give your doe plenty of straw and hay at this time. A nest box (see drawing, page 42) will enhance your doe's sense of well-being, because it will give her the feeling of being safe in a burrow.

Food: The doe's diet should be especially nutritious and varied. You also can give her calcium supplements and

Our dwarf rabbit ought to have some babies. You should let this wish become reality only if you are positive that you can handle the demands that will be placed on you. The chores involved will be time-consuming. In addition, you will have to start early in order to find good homes for the bunnies, assuming you cannot keep all of them.

39

vitamins (available in pet stores). A supply of fresh water should always be within easy reach.

Handling: Pick up the doe only if it is absolutely necessary, especially during the final week of gestation. Do not let her dangle in the air; support her rear end with your other hand immediately upon lifting her.

Behavior with humans: A tame doe will remain friendly during pregnancy and allow herself to be petted. Sometimes, however, she grows nervous and reacts timidly or even aggressively, particularly when faced with strange people or animals. This behavior is normal, however, and it will pass.

Behavior with other rabbits: If you have several female rabbits, keep the pregnant doe housed separately from the others, because she will most likely show aggression toward them. This behavior is not vicious in the least; the rabbit is merely protecting her nesting place (burrow, cage) from rivals. My Mohrle even bit a six-week-old baby rabbit on the nose, something she never would have done otherwise. The doe's behavior toward bucks, however, varies quite widely. Although she will ward off insistent male rabbits (behavior caused by a corpus luteum hormone), she may be altogether tolerant of a castrated male in her vicinity, or of a male whose behavior is not threatening. She will even permit such a rabbit to lick her fur and will snuggle up to him.

Environment: Do not change the cage, and leave it in its customary location. If possible, there should be no stress and no noise, loud music, children shouting and yelling, or banging of doors within the animal's earshot.

Thuringers, five days old.

Birth

Mümmi, our dwarf Thuringer, quite appropriately had her bunnies on Easter Sunday. Naturally, we hoped that the birth process would entail no complications, but I had prepared my children for potential problems. Dwarf does, particularly those producing their first litter, frequently deliver stillborn young. Everything was fine, however, and we were touched as we listened to our three "Easter bunnies," Klösschen, Medi, and Krümel making smacking noises as they began to drink their mother's milk.

Generally, rabbits are alone when they bear their young. Unfortunately, it occasionally happens that the doe partially or entirely eats her babies. Opinions about the causes of this behavior vary. Some experts cite vitamin deficiency; others suspect that the doe, in her extreme eagerness to remove the amniotic sac and bite

If you're only three weeks old, you need a warm nest and plenty of peace and quiet.

through the umbilical cord, simply starts nibbling on the baby too.

   Pointer: See "How To: Raising the Young," pages 42 and 43.

How Often May the Doe Have Young?
Purebred dwarf rabbits generally give birth to no more than two to four young at a time. Through selective breeding, efforts are now being made to increase the average litter size to five or six. Larger litters are obtained when the animals are crossbred with wild rabbits. A healthy rabbit can have two to three litters per year, but a responsible owner and breeder will allow a doe to mate only once or, at most, twice a year.

In the photos:
Newborn bunnies are hairless, blind, and deaf, but by the third week their coats are dense and downy.

HOW–TO
Raising the Young

What happens after birth? What does the doe need? How do the young rabbits develop? What do you do if the mother rabbit dies and you have to raise the young? On these pages, you will find answers to all these questions.

1 A nest box that you can build yourself. The top is hinged.

The Doe after the Birth

Two days after giving birth, Mümmi was her old self again. The extreme nervousness that had appeared during her pregnancy was gone. She clearly enjoyed having us pet her again, and after her daily run she usually lay peacefully in front of her nest box. While she was nursing her bunnies, I fed her three instead of two times a day. The extra food is especially important because nature's primary concern is to

sustain the new life. That is, in order to feed her offspring, the doe needs additional nutrients and vitamins; otherwise, her own reserves will be depleted.

The Development of the Young

Immediately after the kindling, check the nest carefully. Remove any afterbirth remains and any dead rabbits.
If the doe is young and nervous, divert her attention and move her away.

Drawings 1 and 2

The young rabbits lie safe and secure in the nest box, where they are suckled by the doe. The doe does not lie down to nurse her young, but remains in a squatting position while the bunnies lie on their backs beneath her belly and suck. The nursing process is so swift that you will scarcely have a chance to observe it (see "Interesting Facts about Rabbits' Habits," page 59).

How the Young Develop

First week: Newborn rabbits are completely hairless, blind, and deaf. Keeping each other warm, they lie in their nest and are fed by their mother twice a day. The colostrum—the milk secreted immediately after birth—is especially high in protein and contains important antibodies. After each feeding, the doe licks her babies clean and eats their excrement, thus simultaneously stimulating their digestion and keeping the nest clean.
Days 7 to 11: The rabbits' eyes are starting to open now, and their bodies have a soft, downy covering that gives some

idea of the subsequent coat color and markings. After one week, the bunnies' birth weight has doubled, thanks to the high-fat, nutritious doe's milk. It takes 180 days for a human baby's weight to do the same.

Second week: The little rabbits start to crawl; some brave ones even dare to leave the nest. Their fur has become wonderfully thick and soft. They try to clean themselves, but keep losing their balance. They already react to their mother's warning thump and, quick as lightning, look for cover.

2 The doe remains in a squatting position when nursing her young.

Third week: The newborns' trips out of the nest become more frequent. Now they are able to sit up on their hind legs without falling over. They nibble curiously at the hay and straw.
Fourth and fifth weeks: The little rabbits still want to be nursed by their mother, but they also are eating some of the grains, with coarse oat flakes a

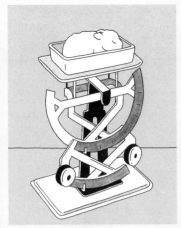

3 Checking a bunny's weight will tell you whether it is gaining regularly.

clear favorite. They can hop on top of their little house and even get up on the sofa. They have become masters of the rabbit's doubling movement, and they play chase-and-catch untiringly. Plenty of exercise from the very beginning will strengthen their hearts, lungs, and muscles and promote the development of their personality and sensory capacities. Rabbits that spend all their time locked in a hutch develop far less well.

From the sixth week on: The young rabbits' gastrointestinal tracts are completely ready for the switch to solid food, but the animals continue to drink their mother's milk, even though it is drying up rapidly.

Eighth week: The young rabbits are big enough to be given away.

Feeding Rabbits from a Bottle
(Drawings 3 and 4)

Unfortunately, it is not uncommon for a mother rabbit to die. If this happens during the first 12 days after the doe gives birth, the prospects for the young rabbits are bleak; if she dies later, they have a chance of survival. If it is not possible for you to put the orphaned bunnies with another lactating doe that will nurse them, you can try to play the role of mother. Don't underestimate the work involved; the duties of a substitute mother for the rabbits are time-consuming.

• Use canned milk with a 10% fat content to feed the young rabbits.

• Get a disposable syringe from your veterinarian. Use it without the needle to feed the rabbits small quantities three to five times a day.

• Hold each tiny animal in your hand for its feeding (see Drawing 4).

• Use your finger to carefully massage each bunny's abdomen in order to stimulate digestion (the doe licks her young after every meal).

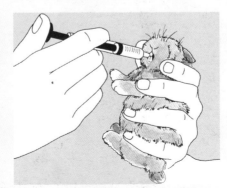

• Keep the bunnies warm (86°F [30°C]). Either keep the room well heated or put a well-wrapped hot-water bottle under the nest.

• After about the third week, you can add thin oat gruel and cooked carrots to their milk.

Important: Weigh the young rabbits regularly to make sure they are gaining the proper amount of weight. If they are not, increase the number of feedings. If necessary, try— through the local rabbit breeders' club, for example—to find a doe that will nurse them.

Tip: If your doe does not have enough milk, you also can use the method previously outlined to help raise the young rabbits.

Healthy, well-fed bunnies lie in their nest with plump tummies. If the bellies of the young rabbits look wrinkled and sunken, you will have to intervene and offer additional food.

4 Hand raising: Hold the bunny like this when you feed it. It is not easy to raise a young rabbit by hand. The bunny has to be fed three to five times a day with the help of a disposable syringe (without a needle).

Dwarf Breeds and Color Varieties

Development of the Breeds

Rabbits have lived with humans for quite a long time. The Romans kept rabbits for their meat, in well-fastened outdoor cages. In those days, however, rabbits were still wild animals. The first tame rabbits appear to have been bred principally in French monasteries. The origins of the development of the breeds have come down to us from sixteenth-century records. The first long-haired rabbits appeared in the early eighteenth century, and in 1874 the first rabbit show was held in Bremen, Germany. Soon rabbit clubs were formed in various European cities, and shortly before the turn of the century a new variety—the dwarf rabbit—appeared among the available breeds. The precursors of the standard dwarf animals we know today came from England. Gradually, through breeding, a true dwarf form was developed that initially weighed as much as 4 pounds 7 ounces (2 kg). In 1940, a Dutchman named Hoefman succeeded in making the first cross between a red-eyed white rabbit and a wild rabbit (see page 50). This dwarf rabbit was smaller and weighed less, but it did not resemble the dwarf form we know today, with the typical bull-like head and small ears.

Characteristics of a Purebred Dwarf

A purebred dwarf rabbit has to display specific characteristics that are laid down by the American Rabbit Breeder's Association (ARBA) and judged at exhibitions. The following guidelines apply to all dwarf breeds, with the exception of the dwarf lop:

Weight: At least 1½ pounds (0.7 kg); ideally, 2½ to 2¾ pounds (1.15–1.25 kg); no more than about 3⅓ pounds (1.5 kg).

Body shape and build: Squat, cylindrical body that is equally broad at the front and the back; short back line, well-rounded hindquarters. The head is large in relation to the body, with a wide forehead and broad muzzle. The forehead should measure 2¼ inches (5.5 cm) across in a buck and 2 inches (5 cm) in a doe. No narrowing is visible between head and body. The eyes are large and "bold," or protruding.

Ears: They should be set close together, nicely rounded at the tips, well-furred, and 1¾ to 2¼ inches (4.5–5.5 cm) long. Ears may be no longer than 2¾ inches (7 cm).

Fur and wool: The fur is judged on its quality and length.

Special breed characteristics: Various colors and types of markings (see pages 46 and 47).

What Is a Standard?

The description of the "ideal" animal of a breed is called the standard. Purebred rabbits are evaluated at exhibitions by the ARBA or the American Netherland Dwarf Rabbit Club (ANDRC). On the following pages I

This three-week-old zebra-colored Jamora is the well-bred son of the mother pictured on the opposite page.

Jamora dwarf Angora.
This zebra-colored bundle of fur is one and a half years old. Like all other Angora rabbits, it has to be clipped regularly.

have described the way the breeds of dwarf rabbits are supposed to look, in terms of their coat (color and markings), claws, and eyes, as specified by the standards. Also provided are the abbreviations that breeders use to designate the breed, color, and markings. (See *The New Rabbit Handbook*, published by Barron's.)

Tattooing: The ears of purebred rabbits are tattooed (see drawing, left).

White Dwarf Rabbits

The red-eyed white dwarf rabbit is the one longest known and best-developed of all the strains. In this breed, we find the animals of the highest quality, with the shortest ears and the most pronounced "bull-shaped" heads. The coat color has to be pure white; it should not have any yellow or gray cast or stains. The claws are colorless; the eyes are either bright red or light blue.

These rabbits, sometimes called "ermine rabbits," are descended from pure-white Polish rabbits that were bred for their fur, which was used as a substitute for the highly coveted but rare ermine pelts. Breeders succeeded in breeding blue-eyed white rabbits as early as 1918, but a long time passed before these animals conformed to the breed standard as closely as present-day red-eyed whites.

Colored Dwarf Rabbits

This category includes all colored dwarf rabbits. Their coat colors correspond in all respects to those of the larger breeds of the color in question. In addition to the colored dwarfs recognized by the ARBA's Standards of Perfection, a number of new breeds have been developed recently, and they are awaiting recognition. We speak of color varieties if a uniform ground color is present, and of vari-

Pedigreed rabbits are tattooed in both ears for easy identification. The numbers in the left ear mean the following: 3 = the month of the animal's birth, March; 1 = 1991, the year of its birth; 35 = its number in the breeder's stock record book.

eties of markings if the animals' various markings or patterns are responsible for their distinctive look.

Color Varieties

Photos on pages 12, 13, and 64

Black: Deep-black coat with no rusty tinge or light spots. Claws dark. Eyes dark brown.

Red: Coat rich fox color, with lighter spots around the eyes and on the chin, jowls, insides of the legs, belly, and tail. Claws dark horn color. Eyes brown.

Havana: Coat shiny dark brown with no gray or rusty tinge. Claws dark horn color. Eyes dark brown, with a reddish gleam.

Chinchilla: Coat makes general impression of being gray, but each individual hair has three bands of color (blue, whitish, and light ash gray). The pelt is streaked with black and black-and-white hairs; the ears are rimmed with black; and the belly and the underside of the tail are white. Claws blackish brown. Eyes dark brown.

Blue: Coat uniformly blue. Claws horn-colored. Eyes blue-gray.

Squirrel gray: Coat evenly blue-gray with dark-tipped and light-tipped guard hairs. Claws horn-colored. Eyes blue-gray.

Agouti or wild (gray): Coat agouti-colored (like that of wild rabbits) with white places on the belly, tail, insides of the legs, and jowls. Claws dark horn-colored. Eyes brown.

Varieties of Markings

Photos on pages 12, 13, and 64

Russian; Black-and-white: Coat snow white with a dark mask that should cover only the nose. Black ears and black "boots." The markings are most distinct in winter (cold-induced darkening); the young are pure white, with coloration beginning to appear after the eighth week. Claws dark brown. Eyes have a red gleam, as in albinos.

Blue-and-white: Blue markings on white ground color.

Thuringer or Thuringer Dwarf: Ground color of coat is chamois, or buff, with bluish-black shading and a dark mask, ears, and "boots"; young are light in color at birth, turning darker later. Claws dark horn color. Eyes brown.

White-tipped Black: Ground color of coat is pure black, with white-tipped guard hairs distributed over the entire body. Belly, inside of legs, underside of tail, eye circles, edges of jowls, nostrils, and ears are a contrasting white. Claws dark, eyes dark brown.

White-tipped Blue: Ground color blue. Eyes blue-gray.

Marten (Yellow or Siamese, Brown, and Blue): Ground colors of coat are light brown (Brown Marten), light blue (Blue Marten), and cream (Yellow Marten, also called Siamese). Dark mask and tail, dark ears, feet, and stripe on the back, shading (successfully bred in Brown Marten) on the haunches and shoulder area. Claws dark (horn-colored in Siamese). Eyes dark brown (blue-gray in Blue Marten).

New Breeds Awaiting Official Recognition

Japanese: Ground color of coat is deep yellow. On both sides there are sharply delineated black stripes (at least four on each flank). Japanese rabbits are most attractive when their head, ears, and front feet are asymmetrically patterned—for example, left side of head yellow with black ear (also may be mottled or marbled), left front foot yellow, right front foot black. Quite difficult to breed because of their markings. Claws dark (horn-colored if the toes are yellow or mottled). Eyes brown.

Tan (Brown-and-tan, Black-and-tan, Blue-and-tan): The top color of the coat is black, brown, or blue; the tanning, which is clearly set off from it, covers the nostrils, jowls, eye circles, edges of the ears, inside of the legs, triangle at the nape of the neck, chest, and belly. Claws dark brown to blackish brown. Eyes brown.

Jamora: Dwarf Angora, a fascinating new breed, still uncommon (see photo, page 44).

Dwarf Lop

The dwarf lop has a special position among dwarf rabbits because of its weight and its drooping ears.

Weight: Up to 4 pounds 6½ ounces (2 kg); the maximum weight for normal dwarf rabbits is 3 pounds 5 ounces (1.5 kg).

Body: Short and cobby; very prominent jowls, broad forehead, ram's nose.

Ears: At the base of the ears are ridges that are suggestive of ram's horns. These ridges gave the breed its German name *Widderzwerg*, or ram dwarf. A lop's ears droop down from the head. In keeping with the dwarf size of this breed, the ears measure only 9½ to 11 inches (24–28 cm). Normal-sized lops have ears 15 to 18 inches (38–45 cm) long.

Coat: Dense and soft. Color varieties as in other dwarf rabbits.

Claws and eyes: In keeping with the coat color.

A *pedigreed rabbit is a rabbit that has been bred by a breeder according to certain guidelines and regulations (stipulated in the standard). At shows, the animal is judged on how closely it conforms to the ideal in various respects. It is graded on size, weight, build, eye color, claw color, and other criteria.*

Crossbred rab-
bits come in a
great variety of
colors and patterns.
If you do not want to
breed rabbits, you
will enjoy a mongrel
just as much as a
purebred rabbit:
They all are lovable.
If you want to be
sure that your
crossbred bunny will
not grow too large
later, make certain
that it resembles a
purebred animal as
closely as possible.

Understanding Rabbits

Rabbits, unlike dogs and cats, are extremely quiet housemates. They do not bark, howl, or meow. Because body language is virtually their only means of expressing pleasure and pain, it is important that you be thoroughly familiar with your pet's patterns of behavior and its needs. Only in this way can you give the rabbit the care it needs and be sure that it feels well.

A Rabbit Is Not a Hare

It is unbelievable how many people confuse rabbits and hares and speak of "dwarf hares." Common hares in dwarf form weighing 2 pounds 14 ounces (1.3 kg) do not exist, however. We still have not succeeded in domesticating hares. They also do not mate with rabbits, and the hare rabbit is only one of the many breeding forms found among purebred rabbits today.

Hares and rabbits differ in a number of ways. The common hare (*Lepus europaeus*) is distinctly a loner who tolerates the company of its kind only when ready for copulation. The hare makes its bed in a shallow hollow (called a "cover") in the ground, where it bears one to four young after a gestation period of about 42 days. Hares are nidifugous; that is, they leave the nest shortly after birth. They are born well-furred and able to see and hear.

Wild rabbits (*Oryctolagus cuniculus*) are gregarious, sociable animals; they like to live together in colonies. They make burrows where they take refuge when enemies appear on the scene and where they bear their young. After a gestation period lasting about 31 days, a wild rabbit gives birth to four to six young, which are completely helpless, naked, blind, and deaf at birth. Baby rabbits are nidicolous animals; they remain in the nest for a period after birth.

Hares and rabbits also differ markedly in their build (see drawing, page 51). The common, or field, hare is a slender, long-legged, long-distance runner that may weigh as much as 13¼ pounds (6 kg). The wild rabbit, on the other hand, has a small, rather compact, muscular body weighing about 2⅕ to 4½ pounds (1–2 kg). It is an agile, skillful short-distance sprinter.

From Wild Rabbit to Household Pet

When the Phoenicians landed on the Iberian Peninsula about 1100 B.C., they found innumerable small, agouti-colored animals darting around among the rocks. On superficial examination, the animals reminded them of the hyraxes that were a familiar sight in their homeland. In reality, these were rabbits, animals as yet unknown to the Phoenicians. Without hesitation, the sailors named the newly discovered land "i-shephan-im"—island of the hyrax. The Latinized name "Hispania" was derived from the Phoenicians' term.

Fossil finds offer proof that large parts of Western Europe were inhabited by wild rabbits long before this time. Displaced during the advent of the Ice Age, the animals moved south into Spain and northwestern Africa. Humans contributed to the further spread of the rabbit: Seafarers took wild rabbits along on their voyages and released them on the islands in the Mediterranean, in Italy, and later in Ireland and England. Wild rabbits reached Germany in the early fifteenth century, but oddly enough, domesticated rabbits already existed there at that time. However that may be, their domestication place took relatively late, in comparison with that of the dog and the cat.

Innate Characteristics of Dwarf Rabbits

Every dwarf rabbit has a white rabbit and a wild rabbit somewhere in its long line of ancestors. No matter how colorful its coat, how short its ears, and how weak its heart, its innate patterns of behavior are the same as those of its distant ancestors, whether it lives in a hutch or in your home.

If you want to understand your little housemate better, familiarize yourself with its natural patterns of behavior and learn to interpret the sounds (see page 53) and body movements (see pages 54 and 55) it makes.

Rabbits are silent companions; this is true in nature also. Wild rabbits have a great many enemies and absolutely no defensive weapons, so they consequently cannot afford to hop around the woods and fields loudly barking, grunting, bellowing, or yowling. Instead, they communicate with each other by using their nose (see page 52) and through body language.

We humans, too, once had more sensitive noses. Expressions such as "he's a stinker" and "he got wind of it" still attest to this.

How Wild Rabbits Live Together

Wild rabbits are social animals. They dig elaborate burrows in which they can take refuge from enemies and raise their young. The social life of the group is conducted there, and the animals are extremely attached to their home. Wild rabbits observe a strict hierarchy. Every colony (eight to fifteen members) is ruled by a dominant buck and a top doe in the roles of king and queen. Only the queen is allowed to raise her young inside the burrow; lower-ranking females have to dig their passageways elsewhere.

Rabbits are peaceable animals.

They fight and quarrel among themselves only when, for example, a pregnant doe is defending her burrow against another female, when young bucks flare up in anger, or when animals of other species try to invade their territory. In such circumstances, these otherwise gentle animals can bite and scratch quite fiercely.

Rabbits are also able to adapt quickly to less suitable accommodations. In areas with damp soil, for instance, they dispense with the digging of burrows and live above ground. In areas that are flooded from time to time, they even live in hollow willow trees. Because of this adaptability, rabbits have become decidedly synanthropic animals; that is, they live in areas developed and cultivated by man. Today they live in parks, gardens, cemeteries, areas near railroad tracks, storage yards, and similar places where humans have left their mark.

A wild rabbit (left) and a hare (right) differ not only in the way they live, but also—as the drawing plainly illustrates—in the shape of their body.

A rabbit's best-developed sensory organ is its nose. Wild rabbits recognize each other outdoors by their smell. Dwarf rabbits, too, recognize their human partners by the scent of their hands, and the animal's sensitive nose registers with dismay the odor of a heavy perfume or a pungent cleaning agent that has been used in cleaning its cage.

Scented Calling Cards

Rabbits have two scent glands that they use to mark objects. One, under the tongue, releases its scent (pheromones)—not detectable to humans—through several pores located beneath the chin. The other gland is near the anus.

Rubbing objects with the chin: This is the rabbit's way of designating its territory and announcing to all other members of its species "I live here. This belongs to me!" Wild rabbits mark rocks, twigs, landmarks, and burrow entries and exits. Rabbits kept as household pets will mark table and chair legs and their cage, food dish, and sleeping house. A rabbit feels safe and at home in surroundings it has marked. Territories that are unmarked or marked by other rabbits, however, make the animal extremely unsure. Dominant bucks and does do the most marking.

Marking with the anus: With their anal gland, rabbits can voluntarily add a secretion to their droppings and thus leave chemical nameplates and calling cards. Scientists have found that rabbits, within their colony, not only recognize each other by their common familiar scent, but also "read" droppings to find out where a rabbit comes from, whether it is male or female, and how old it is. However, wild rabbits can recognize only a limited number of their kind in this way.

Bucks spray their chosen mate with urine to express ownership. Both males and females also spray urine when frightened or as a defensive gesture.

How Wild Rabbits Protect Themselves

Hares and rabbits are commonly believed to be fearful animals. "As timid as a rabbit," we say. But this notion does not quite conform to reality. Although these animals are shy in the wild—they run or hide from their enemies—simple necessity compels them to do so. Otherwise, they would be eaten by weasels, martens, buzzards, hawks, foxes, dogs, or ferrets. All these animals hunt and attack rabbits, which are unable to fend them off because they have no natural defenses. Their only option is to take flight or to crouch and play dead. To put it briefly, rabbits safeguard their existence by fleeing their natural enemies and showing fear.

This behavior is also deeply rooted in tame dwarf rabbits. If a car drives by or an airplane is heard overhead, the rabbit will flatten itself against the floor, with its ears laid back, its eyes wide open, and its body quivering. A wild rabbit, relying on the color of its coat as camouflage, will crouch motionless in the grass until a dangerous bird of prey has flown past. A pet rabbit exhibits similar behavior. It does not "know" that its coat, which may be white, is visible from a great distance, like a flare signal.

Sometimes a sudden noise that is extremely loud will cause a rabbit to take flight in panic. In the close confines of an apartment, such behavior may be dangerous. Otherwise peaceable, even-tempered rabbits may react in this way, particularly if the surroundings are unfamiliar to them. When your pet is allowed to roam free in a meadow, keep its carrier close at hand, so that the rabbit can seek refuge in it. Then the animal will have a chance to explore the new environment bit by bit and, if need be, come back to its sheltering "burrow."

These five-week-old rabbits are eating dandelions, their favorite food, with great relish.

The Language of Sounds

The sounds of wild rabbits, like those of dwarf rabbits, are almost always very soft and tentative. Often you will have to listen very carefully or you won't hear them at all.

Violent gnashing of teeth, in combination with a dull, listless gaze and general apathy: Always a sign of great pain, caused, for example, by tympanitis. Not to be confused with:

Faint grinding noise produced by jaw movement: An expression of contentment, this sound is produced primarily when the back of the rabbit's neck is scratched. It is more pronounced in some rabbits than in others.

Spitting: Always a sign of aggression. A brief spitting sound may precede an attack. It has little similarity to the spitting noises made by cats, however.

Brief growling: This sound usually is produced by bucks shortly after mating.

Cooing: Dwarf does often coo when nursing their young, and rabbits may produce this sound when communicating with each other, if they feel safe, sound, and secure. The range of sounds is quite broad, and the noises are similar to the cooing of doves, although the rabbits' cooing is less even and deeper in pitch.

HOW–TO
Body Language

If you want to thoroughly understand your dwarf rabbit, you will have to learn its body language, because the sounds it makes are few and usually quite soft (see page 53). The more you know about your pet's body language, the fewer mistakes you will make in caring for it.

1 Dwarf rabbits mark objects with the help of a scent gland.

Marking
(Drawing 1)

Frequently you will see your rabbit rubbing its chin on objects. This is a quite natural pattern of behavior. In the wild, rabbits obtain information mainly by using their nose. Consequently, they mark everything that is important to them in order to identify objects and express ownership. They use their scent glands to mark the entries and exits of their burrows, clumps of grass, or posts. In an apartment they will mark,

for example, table and chair legs and their cage, food dish, and sleeping house. The scent is not noticeable to humans.

Ingesting Fecal Pellets
(Drawing 2)

If you see your rabbit eating fecal pellets, don't be alarmed. This behavior, known as coprophagy, is natural and vital to your pet's health. The pellets, excreted by the cecum (the pouch forming the first part of the large intestine), are moist, shiny, and kidney-shaped, not round and dry like normal feces (droppings). Usually eaten immediately upon discharge from the anus, these soft pellets provide the rabbit with essential vitamin B.

Crouching Fearfully
(Drawing 3)

In response to sudden danger or unexpected loud noises, rabbits flatten themselves on the ground and lay their ears back. Watch out when you see your pet in this attitude of concealment: if the rabbit takes flight in panic, it can injure itself.

Alertness
(Drawing 4)

A tense stance, with the tail pointing straight out and the head stretched forward, is a sign of watchfulness, heightened curiosity, and excitement. If the rabbit also puts its ears back, it is ready to attack. Don't touch the animal when this happens; it might bite.

Make a point of explaining this behavioral pattern to your children. All too often, tears and disappointment result when the rabbit suddenly bites without apparent reason.

Other Important Behavior Patterns

The patterns of behavior listed below also are frequently observed in dwarf rabbits:

Sitting up on the hind legs: This posture gives the rabbit a better view of its surroundings—when it is in tall grass, for example. The rabbit also uses this position to reach food it likes. If your rabbit jumps up in the cage and sits up on its hind legs when you approach, it is greeting you and expressing pleasure at the prospect of being let out or fed.

2 Coprophagy, the act of consuming soft fecal pellets, is a normal behavioral pattern for dwarf rabbits, and it is vital to their good health.

Rolling: The animal feels happy. If you put out a box of peat or sand in your house, the dwarf rabbit will likely make this its favorite place to roll. Don't deny your pet this pleasure.

Relaxed squatting with ears laid back: The rabbit wants to rest in peace and quiet. Sometimes it also will graze contentedly. Dwarf rabbits like to spend their "leisure time" in this way.

Lying on one side: The rabbit lies on one side with its legs stretched out, and its eyes slowly begin to close. Now it wants to sleep absolutely undisturbed. When the rabbit is exhausted—in hot weather or after a strenuous run, for example—it will lie down in this position and frequently will also stretch out both legs behind it.

Stretching: Like cats, rabbits are likely to stretch after they rest. This habit is common to all lagomorphic animals, but not to rodents.

Gently nudging with the nose is often simply a gesture of greeting, but it may also be a sign that the rabbit wants to be petted.

Forcefully pushing your hand away is a signal that the animal has had enough petting. Comply with the rabbit's wish; otherwise, you may be nipped.

Licking your hand: This is the rabbit's way of expressing gratitude and contentment. Rabbits that like each other squat close together and lick one another's head.

Stamping and drumming with the hind legs may be an expression of fear, or it may be a threatening or warning ges-

3 If sudden danger looms, rabbits press close to the ground and lay back their ears. You can observe this inborn protective instinct in your indoor rabbit as well.

ture. When enemies approach, wild rabbits thump their hind feet loudly on the ground to warn all their fellows and give the clan a chance to run quickly to the burrow.

Scraping and digging: This is an inborn instinct that your rabbit will try to follow, even indoors. Let your pet scrape and scratch as often as possible: this is the only way to wear down the rabbit's constantly growing claws (see "How To: Care," page 22). However, scraping and digging may have many other meanings. The rabbit may use this gesture to indicate that it wants more attention. It may scratch around in its litter box as a sign that it dislikes the odor there. With does, scraping may be an indication of pregnancy, and some-

times of false pregnancy (see page 39). Aroused males may scratch up the ground—when a rival approaches, for example.

The Importance of Observation

Try to learn the signs that reveal your pet's emotional state, then be sure to watch for these significant behavioral patterns. As you become familiar with rabbit body language, you will become more attuned to your pet and more sensitive to its needs. This can only make the interaction between you more rewarding than ever.

4 A tense body, a tail held horizontal to the ground, and a head stretched forward with ears laid back are indications that the rabbit is ready to attack.

Sniffing and marking objects with the gland in the chin are natural patterns of behavior for rabbits.

Soft or not-so-soft squeaking:
Young rabbits sometimes squeak when they are afraid or hungry. One night I was awakened by this sound to find a newborn rabbit at the foot of my bed, placed there by the doe. I was just in time in laying the bunny back in the warm nest with the others; otherwise, it surely would have died of hypothermia.

Piercing, high-pitched scream:
This cry is uttered only when a rabbit fears for its life or is suffering sudden terrible pain.

Pointer: Since rabbit sounds are very soft and easily missed, it is important to learn the signs that reveal your pet's inner state. See How-To Body Language, pages 54 and 55.

Sensory Capacities

Sight: Wild rabbits see better than hares. Their large eyes, located on the sides of the head, provide them with a wide field of vision, which is crucial to their survival. At twilight, they have relatively good vision. Their ability to see things close at hand, however, is limited because their eyes, like those of many other animals that run from their enemies, are adapted for viewing objects at a distance. You may find that your dwarf rabbit runs right between your legs because of its poor spatial perception and inadequate near vision. When caring for a timid animal with whom you are still unfamiliar, make sure your movements are quiet and deliberate; loud, sudden, or jerky movements may cause the rabbit to flee. In its panicky attempt to get away, the rabbit may injure itself seriously by running into furniture or other objects.

Hearing: With ears that are shaped like elongated funnels, able to swivel independently of one another, dwarf rabbits hear quite well. This ability allows them to hear even the tiniest noises and pinpoint their origin immediately.

Your dwarf rabbit's ears are also highly sensitive to loud noises. The slamming of a door, shouting, the loud barking of a dog, or the shrill, high-pitched calls of nearby birds will most likely scare your pet rabbit and prompt it to flee. Whenever possible, avoid exposing your pet to these noises.

Taste: The rabbit's tongue has approximately 8,000 taste buds. (By way of comparison: a dog's tongue has 48,000.) Although a rabbit prefers certain foods and avoids others, it is unable to detect the presence of poisonous substances readily. Never assume that your dwarf rabbit will be able to tell a poisonous plant from a nonpoisonous one.

This five-week-old rabbit already can sit up on its hind legs.

Touch: Rabbits use their whiskers, which are as long as the animal's body is wide, to gauge the distance to the sides of a burrow's passageways and thereby find their way around underground in the dark. These whiskers (the technical term for them is "vibrissae") are also found above the eyes and on the chin. In addition, the rabbit's entire body is able to perceive tactile stimuli. You can discover this for yourself when caring for your dwarf rabbit: if your pet is agitated, you can calm it down by stroking it gently and carefully.

Smell: A rabbit's most fully developed sense organ is its nose, which is always in motion, sometimes turned up or twisted sideways in a strangely grotesque way. Because the nose has over 100 million olfactory cells, not even the faintest scent escapes its notice. Not surprisingly, both wild rabbits and tame dwarf rabbits communicate by means of their scent. Everywhere they go, they leave their scented calling cards (see page 52). Every day I saw my three dwarf rabbits get into a new "scent fight," apparently waged on the principle that whoever marks last is the winner. As soon as Mohrle hopped away after marking everything thoroughly with her chin gland, for example, Mümmi would rush up and put her own scent marks next to or on top of Mohrle's.

Remarkable Abilities

Wild rabbits are highly adaptable. As the following examples suggest, they are able to adjust in an instant to almost any change in their living conditions.

Birth control: An English researcher named Brambell has done extensive work on a special feature of rabbits' reproduction. He discovered that among wild rabbits, 60 percent of the does' litters are not carried to full term. These are not miscarriages as we understand the term: at a certain stage of the pregnancy, the fetuses gradually disintegrate and are absorbed, or resorbed, by the doe's body. The cause of this strange phenomenon is still not fully understood, but it is generally attributed to certain stressful situations, such as an insufficient food supply or overpopulation in the colony.

Feeding the young: The milk with which the doe nurses her young is so rich in nutrients that a newborn rabbit needs only seven days to double its birth weight, even though it is fed only once or twice a day. By way of comparison: a pig needs 16 days, a horse, 60, and a human, 180.

Adaptation: When searching for food, rabbits can be downright ingenious. On the barren Kerguelen Islands in the Antarctic, they lived on Kerguelen cabbage—a favorite of the whalers as well—because it was all they could find. When it was no longer available, they even made do with seaweed.

Over a period of months, English researchers observed rabbits in marshy areas where reeds and willows grow. To their great surprise, they found that the animals traveled fairly large distances by swimming, although they could have taken a route over land.

In dry, hot Australia, these highly adaptable creatures improved their water equilibrium by means of a four- or fivefold concentration of their urine, thus decreasing the excretion of urine

Rabbits that like each other squat close together and lick each other's head.

and liquids. When they make their burrows, rabbits prefer dry ground where digging is easy; but sometimes they will live in marshy areas also, where they make their home above ground in hollow willow trees.

Interesting Facts about Rabbits' Habits

In an emergency—for example, when being pursued by an enemy—a wild rabbit has to get home safely in a hurry. For this reason, all the habitual paths, the safe, familiar routes to feeding places and back to the burrow, are marked very clearly.

Offspring: Even the smallest members of a wild rabbit's family can use their acute sense of smell to survive. A doe builds her nest burrow some distance away from the main burrow and makes a warm lining for the bottom with fur plucked from her underside. Then she places her young in the nest, scratches dirt over the entrance, and marks it. She slips into the nest only once a day to nurse her offspring. In a matter of seconds, the little creatures—still blind and deaf in the beginning—manage to find their mother's teats by using their sense of smell. Within two minutes they consume enough milk to equal about 25 percent of their body weight. Then the doe leaves them again and covers up the entrance to her nest. It all happens so quickly that an enemy usually does not have time to discover the nest.

Every excess minute the doe spends in the nest burrow, which has only one hole for entry and exit, could make the burrow a death trap for the entire rabbit family. This pattern of behavior is also seen in dwarf rabbits: You will almost never be able to see your pet doe nursing her young.

Exploring the surroundings: Your dwarf rabbit also will mark its paths in your home, on the terrace, or in the yard. It uses this system to find its way around. In completely unfamiliar, unmarked surroundings—on an excursion to the country, for example–

When the rabbit relaxes and stretches out on all fours, it wants to rest in peace and quiet.

the animal will show extreme caution in its behavior. It will repeatedly stand up on its hind legs, move its ears back and forth like TV antennae, and look and sniff all around. Often it will come hopping back to you, because you are its secure place of refuge. If it hears a sudden noise, the rabbit will take flight or flatten itself in the grass with its ears laid back. Everything new is at first a source of stress for the animal. It takes some time before it can be sure that there is no threat of danger, and you always have to allow your pet whatever time it needs (see "Outing in the Country," page 19). Once your dwarf rabbit has investigated the surroundings thoroughly, it will start to hop around happily, cut capers, and gnaw contentedly on some fresh greenery.

Information and Periodicals

The American Rabbit Breeders Association (ARBA)
1925 South Main, Box 426
Bloomington, IL 81701

The ARBA publishes a magazine devoted to the fancy: *Domestic Rabbits*. It contains much useful information on old and new breeds, supplies of stock, and equipment, as well as news about the shows that are held regularly in most parts of the country. An annual subscription is modestly priced, and there are reduced fees for children, senior citizens, and family groups.

Another monthly magazine is: *Rabbits.*
Countryside Publications, Ltd.
312 Portland Road, Highway 19 East
Waterloo, WI 53594

Fanciers of Netherland Dwarf Rabbits have their own organization. For further information, write to the following address:
American Netherland Dwarf Rabbit Club
Donna Decker, Secretary-Treasurer
P.O. Box 99
Mustang, Oklahoma 93064

All serious rabbit fanciers in the United Kingdom should subscribe to the biweekly mazazine *Fur and Feather*, the official magazine of the British Rabbit Council (BRC).

Fur and Feather
British Rabbit Council
Purfoy House
7 Kirkgate
Newark
Nottingham, England

Membership in the BRC is also essential for the English rabbit enthusiast, as this is the governing body of the fancy. The annual subscription fee is small, and there are reduced rates for children, family groups, pensioners, and so on. The official series of rabbit rings supplied by the Council to members helps them maintain records of their stock.

Books

The American Rabbit Breeders Association, *Official Guide to Raising Better Rabbits*, Bloomington, Illinois.
——, *Standard of Perfection: Standard Bred Rabbits and Cavies*, Bloomington, Illinois.
Arrington, L. R., and Kathleen Kelley, *Domestic Rabbit Biology and Production*, University Presses of Florida, Gainesville, Florida.
Downing, Elisabeth, *Keeping Rabbits*, Pelham Books, London, 1979.
Harkness, John, and Joseph Wagner, *The Biology and Medicine of Rabbits and Rodents*, Lea & Febiger, Philadelphia, Pennsylvania, 1988.
Hunter, Samantha, *Hop to It*, Barron's, Hauppauge, New York, 1991.
National Research Council, *Nutrient Requirements of Rabbits*, 2nd edition, National Academy Press, Washington, D.C., 1977.
Sandford, J. C., *The Domestic Rabbit*, Collins, London, 1986.
Vriends-Parent, Lucia, *The New Rabbit Handbook*, Barron's, Hauppauge, New York, 1989.
Wegler, Monika, *Rabbits*, Barron's, Hauppauge, New York, 1990.

Index

Page references in **boldface** type indicate color photos. **C1** indicates front cover; **C2**, inside front cover; **C3**, inside back cover; **C4**, back cover.

Acknowledgments

The author and the publisher are grateful to Dr. Gabriele Wiesner for looking over the chapter "If Your Dwarf Rabbit Gets Sick."

The Photographer and Author

Monika Wegler is the author and photographer of several successful manuals for pet owners. For many years she has worked as a photojournalist for *Das Tier,* a specialized periodical dealing with animals, and for other German and international publications. Her areas of special interest are the keeping, care, breeding, and behavior of rabbits, cats, and dogs.

Front cover: Thuringer.
Back cover: White-tipped Black.

English translation © Copyright 1992 by Barron's Educational Series, Inc.

© Copyright 1991 by Gräfe and Unzer GmbH, Munich, West Germany
The title of the German book is *Zwergkaninchen*

Translated from the German by Kathleen Luft.

All inquiries should be addressed to:
Barron's Educational Series, Inc.
250 Wireless Boulevard
Hauppauge, New York 11788

Library of Congress Catalog Card No. 92-10742

International Standard Book No. 0-8120-1352-2

Library of Congress Cataloging-in-Publication Data

Wegler, Monika.
   [Zwergkaninchen. English]
   Dwarf rabbits : how to take care of them and understand them / Monika Wegler : with color photos by Monika Wegler and drawings by György Jankovics.
      p.   cm.
   Translation of: Zwergkaninchen.
   Includes index.
   ISBN 0-8120-1352-2
   1. Dwarf rabbits.   I. Jankovics, György.
   II. Title.
SF455.D85W4513   1992
636'.9322—dc20   92-10742
                                                             CIP

PRINTED IN HONG KONG
5 4900 987

Important Information

This book deals with the keeping and care of dwarf rabbits as household pets. When handling these animals, you may be scratched or bitten. Such injuries should be treated by a physician without delay. Gnawing is part of the natural behavior of dwarf rabbits. For this reason, it is absolutely essential to supervise dwarf rabbits during their necessary, regular run indoors. To prevent potentially fatal electrical accidents, make sure your pet does not gnaw on any electrical wires.

Some people have allergic reactions to the fur of dwarf rabbits. If in doubt, ask your physician before acquiring a rabbit.

A dwarf rabbit's eyes see better at a distance than up close. Because of its inadequate close vision, the animal may run between your legs and cause you to fall.

Purebreds and Crossbreds

Siamese, 12 weeks old.

Blue, 10 weeks old.

White-tipped Black, six weeks old.

Rabbits, five weeks old.

Red, five weeks old.